simply

Quick and Easy

p

This is a Parragon Publishing book
This edition published in 2002

Parragon Publishing
Queen Street House
4 Queen Street
Bath, BA1 1HE, UK

ISBN: 0-75258-739-0

Printed in China

Produced by The Bridgewater Book Company Ltd.

Art Director: Stephen Knowlden
Editorial Director: Fiona Biggs
Senior Editor: Mark Truman
Editorial Assistant: Tom Kitch
Photography: St John Asprey
Home Economist: Jacqueline Bellefontaine

NOTE
Tablespoons are assumed to be 15 ml.
Unless otherwise stated, milk is assumed
to be whole fat, eggs are medium and pepper
is freshly ground black pepper.

contents

introduction

This book is designed to appeal to anyone who wants a wholesome but quick and easy diet, and includes many recipes suitable for vegetarians and vegans. Its main aim is to show people that, with a little forethought, it is possible to spend very little time in the kitchen while still enjoying appetizing food. The recipes collected together come from all over the world; some of the Indian and barbecue dishes featured require marinating, often overnight, but it is worth remembering that their actual cooking time is very short once the marinade has been absorbed. The more exotic dishes on offer are balanced by some traditional dishes which are sure to become firm family favorites. If you want fast food

for everyday meals, or you are short on time and want to prepare a tasty dinner party treat, there is something for everybody in this book.

To save time in the kitchen, always make sure that you have a stock of staple foodstuffs such as rice, pasta, spices, and herbs, so that you can easily turn your hand to any number of these recipes.

flour

You will need to keep a selection of flour: Self-rising and whole wheat are the most useful. You may also like to keep some rice flour and cornstarch for thickening sauces and to add to cakes, cookies, and puddings. Buckwheat, garbanzo bean, and soya flours can also be bought. These are useful for combining with other flours to add different flavors and a variety of textures.

grains and rice

A good variety of grains is essential. For rice, choose from long-grain, basmati, Italian risotto, short-grain, and wild rice. Look out for fragrant Thai rice, jasmine rice, and combinations of different varieties to add color and texture to your dishes. When choosing your rice, remember that brown rice is a better source of vitamin B1 and fiber.

Other grains add variety to the diet. Try to include some barley millet, bulghur wheat, polenta, oats, semolina, sago, and tapioca.

pasta

Pasta is very popular nowadays, and there are many types and shapes to choose from. Keep a good selection, such as basic lasagne sheets, tagliatelle, fettuccine (flat ribbons), and spaghetti. for a change, sample some of the many fresh pastas now available. Better still, make your own – hand-rolling pasta can be very satisfying, and you can buy a special machine for rolling the dough and cutting certain shapes.

legumes

Legumes are a valuable source of protein, vitamins, and minerals. Stock up on soya beans, navy beans, red kidney beans, cannellini beans, garbanzo beans, lentils, split peas, and butter beans. Buy dried legumes for soaking and cooking yourself, or canned varieties for speed and convenience.

herbs

A good selection of herbs is important for adding variety to your cooking. Fresh herbs are preferable to dried, but it is essential to have dried ones in stock as a useful back-up. You should store dried basil, thyme, bay leaves, oregano, rosemary, mixed herbs, and bouquet garni.

chilies

These come both fresh and dried and in many colors. The hotness varies so use with caution. The seeds are hottest and are usually discarded. Chili powder should also be used sparingly. Check whether the powder is pure chili or a chili seasoning or blend, which should be milder.

nuts and seeds

As well as adding protein, vitamins, and useful fats to the diet, nuts and seeds add important flavor and texture to vegetarian meals. Make sure that you keep a good supply of nuts such as hazelnuts, pine nuts, and walnuts. Coconut is useful too.

For your seed collection, have sesame, sunflower, pumpkin, and poppy. Pumpkin seeds in particular are a good source of zinc.

dried fruits

Currants, raisins, golden raisins, dates, apples, apricots, figs, pears, peaches, prunes, papayas, mangoes, figs, bananas, and pineapples can all be purchased dried and can be used in lots of different recipes. When buying dried fruits, look for untreated varieties: for example, buy figs that have not been rolled in sugar, and choose unsulfured apricots, if they are available.

oils and fats

Oils are useful for adding subtle flavorings to foods, so it is a good idea to have a selection in your cupboard. Use a light olive oil for cooking and extra-virgin olive oil for salad dressings. Use sunflower oil as a good general-purpose oil. Sesame oil is wonderful in stir-fries; hazelnut and walnut oils are superb in salad dressings. Oils and fats add flavor to foods, and contain the important fat-soluble vitamins A, D, E, and K. Remember all fats and oils are high in calories, and that oils are higher in calories than butter or margarine.

vinegars

Choose three or four vinegars – red or white wine, cider, light malt, tarragon, sherry, or balsamic vinegar, to name just a few. Each will add its own character to your recipes.

mustards

Mustards are made from black, brown, or white mustard seeds which are ground and mixed with spices. Meaux mustard is made from mixed mustard seeds and has a grainy texture with a warm taste. Dijon mustard, made from husked and ground mustard seeds, has a sharp flavor. Its versatility in salads and with grills makes it ideal for the vegetarian. German mustard is mild and is best used in Scandinavian and German dishes.

bottled sauces

Soy sauce is widely used in Eastern cookery and is made from fermented yellow soya beans mixed with wheat, salt, yeast, and sugar. Light soy sauce tends to be rather salty, whereas dark soy sauce tends to be sweeter. Teriyaki sauce gives an authentic Japanese flavor to stir-fries. Black bean and yellow bean sauces add an instant authentic Chinese flavor to stir-fries.

storing spices

Your basic stock of spices should include fresh gingerroot and garlic, chili powder, turmeric, paprika, cloves, cardamom, black pepper, ground coriander, and ground cumin. The powdered spices will keep very well in airtight containers, while the fresh gingerroot and garlic will keep for 7-10 days in the refrigerator. Other useful items, to be acquired as your repertoire increases, are cumin seeds (black as well as white), onion seeds, mustard seeds, cloves, cinnamon, dried red chilies, fenugreek, vegetable ghee and garam masala (a mixture of spices that can either be bought ready-made or made at home in quantity for use whenever required).

using spices

You can use spices whole, ground, roasted, fried, or mixed with yogurt to marinate meat and poultry. One spice can alter the flavor of a dish and a combination of several can produce different colors and textures. The quantities of spices shown in the recipes are merely a guide. Increase or decrease them as you wish, especially in the cases of salt and chili powder, which are a matter of taste.

Many of the recipes in this book call for ground spices, which are generally available in stores as well as in Indian and Pakistani grocers. In India whole spices are ground at home, and there is no doubt that freshly ground spices do make a noticeable difference to the taste.

Some recipes require roasted spices. In India, this is done on a thawa, but you can use a heavy, ideally cast-iron skillet. No water or oil is needed: the spices are simply dry-roasted whole while the pan is shaken to stop them burning on the bottom.

Remember that long cooking over a lowish heat will improve the taste of the food as it allows the spices to be absorbed. This is why reheating dishes the following day is no problem for most Indian food.

useful oriental ingredients

Bamboo shoots
These are added for texture, as they have very little flavor. Available in cans, they are a common ingredient in Chinese cooking.

Beansprouts
These are mung bean shoots, which are very nutritious, containing many vitamins. They add crunch to a recipe and are widely available. Do not overcook them, as they wilt and do not add texture to the dish.

Black beans
These are soy beans and are very salty. They can be bought and crushed with salt and then rinsed or used in the form of a ready-made sauce for convenience.

Chinese beans
These long beans may be eaten whole and are very tender. Green beans may also be used.

Chinese five-spice powder
An aromatic blend of cinnamon, cloves, star anise, fennel, and brown peppercorns. It is often used in marinades.

Chinese leaves
A light green leaf with a sweet flavor. It can be found readily in most supermarkets.

Hoisin sauce
A dark brown, sweet, thick sauce that is widely available. It is made from spices, soy sauce, garlic, and chili and is often served as a dipping sauce.

Lychees
These are worth buying fresh, as they are easy to prepare. Inside the inedible skin is a fragrant white fruit. Lychees are available canned and are a classic Chinese ingredient.

Mango
Choose a ripe mango for its sweet, scented flesh. If a mango is underripe when bought, leave it in a sunny place for a few days before using.

Noodles
The Chinese use several varieties of noodle. You will probably find it easier to use the readily available dried varieties, such as egg noodles, which are yellow, rice-stick noodles, which are white and very fine, or transparent noodles, which are opaque when dry and turn transparent on cooking. However, cellophane or rice noodles may be used instead.

Oyster sauce
Readily available, this sauce is made from oysters, salt, seasonings, and cornstarch and is brown in color.

Pak choi
Also known as Chinese cabbage, this has a mild, slightly bitter flavor.

Rice vinegar
This has a mild, sweet taste that is quite delicate. It is available in some supermarkets, but if not available use cider vinegar instead.

Rice wine
This is similar to dry sherry in color, alcohol content, and smell, but it is worth buying rice wine for its distinctive flavor.

Sesame oil
This is made from roasted sesame seeds and has an intense flavor. It burns easily and is therefore added at the end of cooking for flavor, and is not used for frying.

Soy sauce
This is widely available, but it is worth buying a good grade of sauce. It is produced in both light and dark varieties – the former is used with fish and vegetables for a lighter color and flavor, while the latter, being darker, richer, saltier, and more intense, is used as a dipping sauce or with strongly flavored meats.

Star anise
This is an eight-pointed, star-shaped pod with a strong aniseed flavor. The spice is also available ground. If a pod is added to a dish, it should be removed before serving.

Szechuan pepper
This is quite hot and spicy and should be used sparingly. It is red in color and is readily available.

Tofu or bean curd
This soya bean paste is available in several forms. The cake variety, which is soft and spongy and a white-gray color, is used in this book. It is very bland, but adds texture to dishes and is perfect for absorbing all the other flavors in the dish.

Water chestnuts
These are flat and round and can usually only be purchased in cans, already peeled. They add a delicious crunch to dishes and have a sweet flavor.

Yellow beans
Again a soy bean and very salty. Use a variety that is chunky rather than smooth.

A tasty soup or appetizer that complements the dishes to follow can help set the tone for the rest of a meal, and the wide variety of dishes in this section offer a host of options to match almost any main course. The soups can also be light meals in themselves, served with fresh bread, and many of the starters can be served as side dishes or snacks. One of the great strengths of soups is their versatility. Although the best

results are obtained from using fresh ingredients, soups are a still a quick and easy way of using up leftovers. Soup recipes can also be stretched to serve more people simply by increasing the amount of bouillon used. They can be thickened by adding more vegetables. If you have the

time, making your own bouillon is a healthy alternative to using granules or bouillon cubes which can contain salt and flavorings and may have too strong a taste.

soups
& appetizers

dal soup

Dal is the name given to a delicious Indian lentil dish. This soup is a variation of the theme—it is made with red lentils and spiced with curry powder.

Serves 4

2 tbsp butter

2 garlic cloves, finely chopped

1 onion, chopped

½ tsp turmeric

1 tsp garam masala

¼ tsp chili powder

1 tsp ground cumin

2 lb canned, chopped tomatoes, drained

1 cup red lentils

2 tsp lemon juice

2½ cups vegetable stock

1¼ cups coconut milk

salt and pepper

chopped cilantro and lemon slices,
   to garnish

naan bread, to serve

1

2

2

1 Melt the butter in a large pan and sauté the garlic and onion for 2–3 minutes, stirring. Add the spices and cook for a further 30 seconds.

2 Stir in the tomatoes, red lentils, lemon juice, vegetable stock, and coconut milk and bring to a boil.

3 Reduce the heat and simmer for 25–30 minutes until the lentils are tender and cooked.

4 Season to taste and spoon the soup into a warm tureen. Garnish and serve with warm naan bread.

cook's tip

You can buy cans of coconut milk from stores and delicatessens. It can also be made by grating creamed coconut, which comes in the form of a solid bar, and mixing it with water.

cook's tip

Add small quantities of hot water to the pan whilst the lentils are cooking if they begin to absorb too much of the liquid.

broccoli & potato soup

This creamy soup has a delightful pale green coloring and rich flavor from the blend of tender broccoli and blue cheese.

1 Heat the oil in a large pan and add the diced potatoes and onion. Sauté gently for 5 minutes, stirring constantly.

Serves 4

2 tbsp olive oil

2 potatoes, diced

1 onion, diced

8 oz broccoli flowerets

4½ oz blue cheese, crumbled

4½ cups vegetable stock

½ cup heavy cream

pinch of paprika

salt and pepper

2 Reserve a few broccoli flowerets for the garnish and add the remaining broccoli to the pan. Add the cheese and stock.

3 Bring to a boil, then reduce the heat, cover the pan and simmer for 25 minutes until the potatoes are tender.

4 Transfer the soup to a food processor or blender in 2 batches and process until the mixture is a smooth purée.

5 Return the purée to a clean pan and stir in the cream and a pinch of paprika. Season to taste with salt and pepper.

6 Blanch the reserved broccoli flowerets in a little boiling water for about 2 minutes, then drain with a draining spoon.

7 Pour the soup into warmed bowls and garnish with the broccoli flowerets and a sprinkling of paprika. Serve immediately.

1

5

6

cook's tip

This soup freezes very successfully. Follow the method described here up to step 4, and freeze the soup after it has been puréed. Add the cream and paprika just before serving. Garnish and serve.

indian potato & pea soup

A slightly hot and spicy Indian flavor is given to this soup with the use of garam masala, chili, cumin, and coriander.

2

Serves 4

2 tbsp vegetable oil

8 oz mealy potatoes, diced

1 large onion, chopped

2 garlic cloves, finely chopped

1 tsp garam masala

1 tsp ground coriander

1 tsp ground cumin

3¾ cups vegetable stock

1 red chili, chopped

3½ oz frozen English peas

4 tbsp unsweetened yogurt

salt and pepper

chopped fresh cilantro, to garnish

1 Heat the vegetable oil in a large pan and add the diced potatoes, onion, and garlic. Sauté gently for about 5 minutes, stirring constantly.

2 Add the ground spices and cook for 1 minute, stirring all the time.

3 Stir in the vegetable stock and chopped red chili and bring the mixture to a boil. Reduce the heat, cover the pan and simmer for 20 minutes until the potatoes begin to break down.

4 Add the peas and cook for a further 5 minutes. Stir in the yogurt and season to taste.

5 Pour into warmed soup bowls, garnish with chopped fresh cilantro and serve hot with warm bread.

cook's tip

Potatoes blend perfectly with spices, this soup being no exception. For an authentic Indian dish, serve this soup with warm naan bread.

variation

For slightly less heat, seed the chili before adding it to the soup. Always wash your hands after handling chilies as they contain volatile oils that can irritate the skin and make your eyes burn if you touch your face.

3

4

tuscan onion soup

This soup is best made with white onions, which have a milder flavor than the more usual brown variety. If you cannot get hold of them, try using large Spanish onions instead.

Serves 4

1¾ oz pancetta ham, diced

1 tbsp olive oil

4 large white onions,
    sliced thinly in rings

3 garlic cloves, chopped

3¾ cups hot chicken or ham stock

4 slices ciabatta or other Italian bread

3 tbsp butter

2¾ oz Gruyère or Cheddar cheese

salt and pepper

cook's tip

Pancetta is similar to bacon, but it is air and salt-cured for about 6 months. Pancetta is available from most delicatessens and some large stores. If you cannot obtain pancetta use unsmoked bacon instead.

1 Dry fry the pancetta in a large pan for 3–4 minutes until it begins to brown. Remove the pancetta from the pan and set aside until required.

1

2

2 Add the oil to the pan and cook the onions and garlic over a high heat for 4 minutes. Reduce the heat, cover and cook for 15 minutes until lightly caramelized.

3 Add the stock to the pan and bring to a boil. Reduce the heat and leave the mixture to simmer, covered, for about 10 minutes.

4 Toast the slices of ciabatta on both sides, under a preheated broiler, for 2–3 minutes or until golden. Spread the ciabatta with butter and top with the Gruyère or Cheddar cheese. Cut the bread into bite-size pieces.

5 Add the reserved pancetta to the soup and season to taste with salt and pepper. Pour into 4 soup bowls and top with the toasted bread.

4

celery, stilton, & walnut soup

This is a classic combination of ingredients all brought together in a delicious, creamy soup. Serve with whole wheat bread for a light lunch.

Serves 4

4 tbsp butter

2 shallots, chopped

3 celery stalks, chopped

1 garlic clove, finely chopped

2 tbsp all-purpose flour

2½ cups vegetable stock

1¼ cups milk

1½ cups blue Stilton cheese, crumbled, plus
    extra to garnish

2 tbsp walnut halves, roughly chopped

½ cup unsweetened yogurt

salt and pepper

chopped celery leaves, to garnish

1 Melt the butter in a large pan and
  sauté the shallots, celery, and garlic
for 2–3 minutes, stirring, until soft.

2 Add the flour and cook
  for 30 seconds.

3 Gradually stir in the vegetable stock
  and milk and bring to a boil.

4 Reduce the heat to a simmer
  and add the crumbled blue Stilton
cheese and walnut halves. Cover and
simmer for 20 minutes.

2

5

5 Stir in the unsweetened yogurt
  and heat for a further 2 minutes
without boiling.

6 Season the soup, then transfer to
  a warm soup tureen or individual
serving bowls, garnish with chopped
celery leaves and extra crumbled blue
Stilton cheese and serve at once.

4

variation

Use an alternative blue
cheese, such as Dolcelatte
or Gorgonzola, if preferred
or a strong vegetarian Cheddar
cheese, grated.

cook's tip

As well as adding protein,
vitamins, and useful fats to
the diet, nuts add important
flavor and texture to
vegetarian meals.

green soup

This fresh-tasting soup with dwarf beans, cucumber, and watercress can be served warm or chilled on a hot summer day.

Serves 4

1 tbsp olive oil

1 onion, chopped

1 garlic clove, chopped

7 oz potato, peeled and cut into
    1 inch cubes

scant 3 cups vegetable or chicken stock

1 small cucumber or ½ large cucumber, cut
    into chunks

3 oz bunch watercress

4½ oz dwarf beans, trimmed and halved
    in length

salt and pepper

variation

Try using 4½ oz snow peas
instead of the beans, if
you prefer.

2

3

1 Heat the oil in a large pan and sauté the onion and garlic for 3–4 minutes or until soft. Add the cubed potato and cook for a further 2–3 minutes.

2 Stir in the stock, bring to a boil and leave to simmer for 5 minutes.

3 Add the cucumber to the pan and cook for a further 3 minutes or until the potatoes are tender. Test by inserting the tip of a knife into the potato cubes – it should pass through easily.

4 Add the watercress and allow to wilt. Then place the soup in a food processor and blend until smooth. Alternatively, before adding the water-cress, mash the soup with a potato masher and push through a strainer, then chop the watercress finely and stir into the soup.

4

5 Bring a small pan of water to a boil and steam the beans for 3–4 minutes or until tender.

6 Add the beans to the soup, season and warm through.

orange, thyme, & pumpkin soup

This thick, creamy soup has a wonderful, warming golden color.
It is flavored with orange and thyme.

1

2

Serves 4

2 tbsp olive oil

2 medium onions, chopped

2 cloves garlic, chopped

2 lb pumpkin, peeled and cut into
  1 inch chunks

6¼ cups boiling vegetable or
  chicken stock

finely grated rind and juice of 1 orange

3 tbsp fresh thyme, stalks removed

¼ cup milk

salt and pepper

crusty bread, to serve

4

1 Heat the olive oil in a large pan. Add the onions to the pan and sauté for 3–4 minutes or until soft. Add the garlic and pumpkin and cook for a further 2 minutes, stirring well.

2 Add the boiling vegetable or chicken stock, orange rind and juice, and 2 tablespoons of the thyme to the pan. Leave to simmer, covered, for 20 minutes or until the pumpkin is tender.

3 Place the mixture in a food processor and blend until smooth.

cook's tip

Pumpkins are usually large vegetables. To make things a little easier, ask the grocer to cut a chunk off for you. Alternatively, make double the quantity and freeze the soup for up to 3 months.

Alternatively, mash the mixture with a potato masher until smooth. Season to taste with salt and pepper.

4 Return the soup to the pan and add the milk. Reheat the soup for 3–4 minutes or until it is very hot but not boiling. Sprinkle with the remaining fresh thyme just before serving.

5 Divide the soup among 4 warm soup bowls and serve with lots of fresh crusty bread.

potato, cabbage, & chorizo soup

Chorizo is a spicy sausage originating from Spain where it is used to add its unique strong flavor to enhance many traditional dishes.

1

4

Serves 4

2 tbsp olive oil

3 large potatoes, cubed

2 red onions, quartered

1 garlic clove, finely chopped

4½ cups pork or vegetable stock

5½ oz Savoy cabbage, shredded

1¼ oz chorizo sausage, sliced

salt and pepper

paprika, to garnish

1 Heat the olive oil in a large pan and add the cubed potatoes, quartered red onions, and garlic. Sauté gently for 5 minutes, stirring constantly.

2 Add the pork or vegetable stock and bring to a boil. Reduce the heat and cover the pan. Simmer the vegetables for about 20 minutes until the potatoes are tender.

3 Process the soup in a food processor or blender in 2 batches for 1 minute each. Return the puréed soup to a clean pan.

4 Add the shredded Savoy cabbage and sliced chorizo sausage to the pan and cook for a further 7 minutes. Season to taste.

5 Ladle the soup into warmed soup bowls, garnish with a sprinkling of paprika and serve.

variation

If chorizo sausage is not available, you could use any other spicy sausage or even salami in its place.

cook's tip

Chorizo sausage requires no pre-cooking. In this recipe, it is added towards the end of the cooking time so that it does not overpower the other flavors in the soup.

brown lentil soup with pasta

In Italy, this soup is called Minestrade Lentiche. A minestra is a soup cooked with pasta; in this case farfalline, a small bow-shaped variety, is used. Served with lentils, this hearty soup is a meal in itself.

Serves 4

4 rashers sliced bacon, cut into small squares

1 onion, chopped

2 garlic cloves, finely chopped

2 celery stalks, chopped

¼ cup farfalline or spaghetti broken into small pieces

1 x 14½ oz can brown lentils, drained

5 cups hot ham or vegetable stock

2 tbsp chopped, fresh mint

variation

Any type of pasta can be used in this recipe. Try fusilli, conchiglie, or rigatoni, if you prefer.

cook's tip

If you prefer to use dried lentils, add the stock before the pasta and cook for 1-1¼ hours until the lentils are tender. Add the pasta and cook for a further 12-15 minutes.

1

2

3

1 Place the bacon in a large skillet together with the onion, garlic, and celery. Dry fry for 4–5 minutes, stirring, until the onion is tender and the bacon is just beginning to brown.

2 Add the farfalline or spaghetti pieces to the skillet and cook, stirring, for about 1 minute to coat the pasta in the oil.

3 Add the lentils and the stock and bring to a boil. Reduce the heat and leave to simmer for 12–15 minutes or until the pasta is tender.

4 Remove the skillet from the heat and stir in the chopped fresh mint.

5 Transfer the soup to warm soup bowls and serve immediately.

tuscan bean & vegetable soup

This thick, satisfying blend of beans and diced vegetables in a rich red wine and tomato stock, based on an Italian favorite, makes an ideal simple supper.

Serves 4

1 medium onion, chopped

1 garlic clove, finely chopped

2 celery stalks, sliced

1 large carrot, diced

14 oz can chopped tomatoes

⅔ cup Italian red wine

5 cups fresh vegetable stock

1 tsp dried oregano

15 oz can mixed beans
    and legumes

2 medium zucchini, diced

1 tbsp tomato paste

salt and pepper

pesto sauce (see page 310
    or use shop-bought) and crusty bread,
    to serve

variation

For a more substantial soup, add 12 oz diced lean cooked chicken or turkey with the tomato paste in step 3.

1

2

3

1 Place the prepared onion, garlic, celery, and carrot in a large pan. Stir in the tomatoes, red wine, vegetable stock, and oregano.

2 Bring the vegetable mixture to a boil, cover, and leave to simmer for 15 minutes. Stir the beans and zucchini into the mixture, and continue to cook, uncovered, for a further 5 minutes.

3 Add the tomato paste to the mixture and season well with salt and pepper to taste. Then heat through, stirring occasionally, for a further 2–3 minutes, but do not allow the mixture to boil again.

4 Ladle the soup into warm bowls and serve with a spoonful of pesto on each portion and accompanied with crusty bread.

sweet potato & onion soup

This simple recipe uses the sweet potato with its distinctive flavor and color as the base for a delicious soup with a hint of orange and cilantro.

Serves 4

2 tbsp vegetable oil

2 lb sweet potatoes, diced

1 carrot, diced

2 onions, sliced

2 garlic cloves, finely chopped

2½ cups vegetable stock

1¼ cups unsweetened orange juice

1 cup unsweetened yogurt

2 tbsp chopped fresh cilantro

salt and pepper

cilantro sprigs and orange rind, to garnish

1

2

5

4 Transfer the mixture to a food processor or blender in batches and process for 1 minute until puréed. Return the purée to the rinsed-out pan.

cook's tip

This soup can be chilled before serving, if preferred. If chilling it, stir the yogurt into the dish just before serving. Serve in chilled bowls.

1 Heat the vegetable oil in a large pan and add the diced sweet potatoes and carrot, sliced onions, and garlic. Sauté gently for 5 minutes, stirring constantly.

2 Pour in the vegetable stock and orange juice and bring them to a boil.

3 Reduce the heat to a simmer, cover the pan and cook the vegetables for 20 minutes or until the sweet potato and carrot cubes are tender.

5 Stir in the unsweetened yogurt and chopped cilantro and season to taste. Serve the soup garnished with cilantro sprigs and orange rind.

creamy tomato soup

This quick and easy creamy soup has a lovely fresh tomato flavor.

Serves 4

3 tbsp butter

1 lb 9oz ripe tomatoes, preferably plum,
  roughly chopped

salt and pepper

3¾ hot vegetable stock

⅔ cup milk or light cream

¼ cup ground almonds

1 tsp sugar

2 tbsp shredded basil leaves

1. Melt the butter in a large pan. Add the tomatoes and cook for 5 minutes until the skins start to wrinkle. Season to taste with salt and pepper.

2. Add the stock to the pan, bring to a boil, cover, and simmer for 10 minutes.

3. Meanwhile, under a preheated broiler, lightly toast the ground almonds until they are golden-brown. This will take only 1-2 minutes, so watch them closely.

4. Remove the soup from the heat and place in a food processor and blend the mixture to form a smooth consistency. Alternatively, mash the soup with a potato masher.

5. Pass the soup through a strainer to remove any tomato skin or pips.

6. Place the soup in the pan and return to the heat. Stir in the milk or cream, ground almonds, and sugar. Warm the soup through and add the shredded basil just before serving.

7. Transfer the creamy tomato soup to warm soup bowls and serve hot.

variation

Very fine bread crumbs can be used instead of the ground almonds, if you prefer. Toast them in the same way as the almonds and add with the milk or cream in step 6.

red bell pepper & chili soup

This soup has a real Mediterranean flavor, using sweet red bell peppers, tomato, chili and basil. It is great served with a warm olive bread.

1

3

4

Serves 4

8 oz red bell peppers,
    seeded and sliced

1 onion, sliced

2 garlic cloves, finely chopped

1 green chili, chopped

1½ cups sieved tomatoes

2½ cups vegetable stock

2 tbsp chopped basil

fresh basil sprigs, to garnish

1 Put the bell peppers in a large pan with the onion, garlic, and chili. Add the sieved tomatoes and vegetable stock and bring to a boil, stirring well.

2 Reduce the heat to a simmer and cook for 20 minutes or until the bell peppers have softened. Drain, reserving the liquid and vegetables separately.

3 Strain the vegetables by pressing through a strainer with the back of a spoon. Alternatively, blend in a food processor until smooth.

4 Return the vegetable purée to a clean pan with the reserved cooking liquid. Add the basil and heat through until hot. Garnish the soup with fresh basil sprigs and serve.

variation

This soup is also delicious served cold with ¾ cup of unsweetened yogurt swirled into it.

cook's tip

Basil is a useful herb to grow at home. It can be grown easily in a window box.

vegetable soup with cannelini beans

This wonderful combination of beans, vegetables, and vermicelli is made even richer by the addition of pesto and dried mushrooms.

Serves 4

1 small eggplant

2 large tomatoes

1 potato, peeled

1 carrot, peeled

1 leek

14½ oz can cannelini beans

3¾ cups hot vegetable or chicken stock

2 tsp dried basil

½ oz dried porcini mushrooms,
    soaked for 10 minutes in enough warm
    water to cover

¼ cup vermicelli

3 tbsp pesto (see page 310 or use
    shop bought)

freshly grated Parmesan cheese, to serve
    (optional)

2

3

cook's tip

Porcini are a wild mushroom
grown in southern Italy. When
dried and rehydrated they have
a very intense flavor, so
although they are expensive
to buy, only a small amount
is required to add flavor
to soups or risottos.

6

1 Slice the eggplant into rings about
½ inch thick, then cut each ring into 4.

2 Cut the tomatoes and potato into
small dice. Cut the carrot into sticks,
about 1 inch long and cut the leek
into rings.

3 Place the cannelini beans and their
liquid in a large pan. Add the
eggplant, tomatoes, potatoes, carrot,
and leek, stirring to mix.

4 Add the stock to the pan and bring
to a boil. Reduce the heat and leave
to simmer for 15 minutes.

5 Add the basil, dried mushrooms,
their soaking liquid, and the
vermicelli and simmer for 5 minutes or
until all of the vegetables are tender.

6 Remove the pan from the heat and
stir in the pesto.

7 Serve with freshly grated Parmesan
cheese, if using.

cream of chicken & tomato soup

This soup is very good made with fresh tomatoes, but if you prefer, you can use canned tomatoes, although the flavor will not be as good.

2

4

Serves 2

4 tbsp unsalted butter

1 large onion, chopped

1 lb chicken, shredded very finely

2½ cups chicken stock

6 medium tomatoes, chopped finely

pinch of baking soda

salt and pepper

1 tbsp superfine sugar

⅔ cup heavy cream

fresh basil leaves, to garnish

croutons, to serve

1 Melt the butter in a large pan and sauté the onion and shredded chicken for 5 minutes.

2 Add 1¼ cups chicken stock to the pan, with the tomatoes and baking soda.

3 Bring the soup to a boil and simmer for 20 minutes.

4 Allow the soup to cool, then blend in a food processor.

5 Return the soup to the pan, add the remaining chicken stock, season, and add the sugar. Pour the soup into a tureen and add a swirl of heavy cream. Serve the soup with croutons and garnish with basil.

5

cream of chicken soup

Tarragon adds a delicate aniseed flavor to this tasty soup.
If you can't find tarragon, use parsley for a fresh taste.

Serves 4

4 tbsp unsalted butter

1 large onion, peeled and chopped

10½ oz cooked chicken,
    shredded finely

2½ cups chicken stock

salt and pepper

1 tbsp chopped fresh tarragon

⅔ cup heavy cream

fresh tarragon leaves, to garnish

deep fried croutons, to serve

1 Melt the butter in a large pan and sauté the onion for 3 minutes.

2 Add the chicken to the pan with 1¼ cups of the chicken stock.

3 Bring to a boil and simmer for 20 minutes. Allow to cool, then liquidize the soup.

4 Add the remainder of the stock and season with salt and pepper.

5 Add the chopped tarragon, pour the soup into a tureen or individual serving bowls, and add a swirl of cream.

6 Garnish the soup with fresh tarragon and serve with deep fried croutons.

5

1

2

variation

To make garlic croutons, grind 3-4 garlic cloves in a mortar and pestle and add to the oil.

variation

If you can't find fresh tarragon, freeze-dried tarragon makes a good substitute. Light cream can be used instead of the heavy cream.

chicken & corn soup

This heart-warming soup is both quick and easy to make.

Serves 4

1 lb boned chicken breasts, cut into strips

5 cups chicken stock

⅔ cup heavy cream

salt and pepper

¾ cup dried vermicelli

1 tbsp cornstarch

3 tbsp milk

6 oz corn kernels

variation

For crab and corn soup,
substitute 1 lb cooked
crabmeat for the chicken
breasts. Flake the crabmeat
well before adding it to
the pan and reduce the cooking
time by 10 minutes. For a
Chinese-style soup, substitute
egg noodles for the vermicelli
and use canned, creamed corn.

1

1 Put the chicken, stock, and cream
into a large pan and bring to a boil
over a low heat. Reduce the heat slightly
and simmer for about 20 minutes.
Season the soup with salt and pepper
to taste.

2 Meanwhile, cook the vermicelli in
lightly salted boiling water for 10-12
minutes, until just tender. Drain the pasta
and keep warm.

3 In a small bowl, mix together the
cornstarch and milk to make a
smooth paste. Stir the cornstarch into
the soup until thickened.

4 Add the corn and vermicelli to the
pan and heat through.

5 Transfer the soup to a warm
tureen or individual soup bowls and
serve immediately.

4

4

cook's tip

If you are short of time,
buy ready-cooked chicken,
remove any skin and cut it
into slices.

chinese potato & pork broth

In this recipe the pork is seasoned with traditional Chinese flavorings—soy sauce, rice-wine vinegar, and a dash of sesame oil.

Serves 4

4½ cups chicken stock

2 large potatoes, diced

2 tbsp rice-wine vinegar

2 tbsp cornstarch

4 tbsp water

4½ oz pork tenderloin, sliced

1 tbsp light soy sauce

1 tsp sesame oil

1 carrot, cut into very thin strips

1 tsp gingerroot, chopped

3 scallions, sliced thinly

1 red bell pepper, sliced

8 oz can bamboo shoots, drained

1 Add the chicken stock, diced potatoes, and 1 tbsp of the rice-wine vinegar to a pan and bring to a boil. Reduce the heat until the stock is just simmering.

2 In a small bowl, mix the cornstarch with the water. Stir the mixture into the hot stock.

3 Bring the stock back to a boil, stirring until thickened, then reduce the heat until it is just simmering again.

4 Place the pork in a shallow dish and season with the remaining rice-wine vinegar, soy sauce and sesame oil.

5 Add the pork slices, carrot strips, and chopped gingerroot to the stock and cook for 10 minutes. Stir in the sliced scallions, red bell pepper, and bamboo shoots. Cook for a further 5 minutes.

6 Pour the soup into warmed bowls and serve immediately.

5

4

5

variation

For extra heat, add 1 chopped red chili or 1 tsp of chili powder to the soup in step 5.

cook's tip

Sesame oil is very strongly flavored and is, therefore, only used in small quantities.

lamb & rice soup

This is a very filling soup, as it contains rice and tender pieces of lamb.
Serve before a light main course.

Serves 4

5½ oz lean lamb

salt

¼ cup rice

3¾ cups lamb stock

1 leek, sliced

1 garlic clove, thinly sliced

2 tsp light soy sauce

1 tsp rice-wine vinegar

1 medium open-cap mushroom, sliced

2

4

5

1 Using a sharp knife, trim any fat from the lamb and cut the meat into thin strips. Set aside until required.

2 Bring a large pan of lightly salted water to a boil and add the rice. Bring back to a boil, stir once, reduce the heat and cook for 10–15 minutes, until tender. Drain, rinse under cold running water, drain again, and set aside until required.

3 Meanwhile, put the lamb stock in a large pan and bring to a boil.

4 Add the lamb strips, leek, garlic, soy sauce, and rice-wine vinegar to the stock in the pan. Reduce the heat, cover and leave to simmer for 10 minutes, or until the lamb is tender and cooked through.

5 Add the mushroom slices and the rice to the pan and cook for a further 2–3 minutes, or until the mushroom is completely cooked through.

6 Ladle the soup into 4 individual soup bowls and serve immediately.

cook's tip

Use a few dried Chinese mushrooms, rehydrated according to the packet instructions and chopped, as an alternative to the open-cap mushroom. Add the Chinese mushrooms with the lamb in step 4.

beef & vegetable noodle soup

Thin strips of beef are marinated in soy sauce and garlic to form the basis of this tasty soup. Served with noodles, it is both filling and delicious.

Serves 4

8 oz lean beef

1 garlic clove, finely chopped

2 scallions, chopped

3 tbsp soy sauce

1 tsp sesame oil

8 oz egg noodles

3¾ cups beef stock

3 baby corn, sliced

½ leek, shredded

4½ oz broccoli, cut into flowerets

pinch of chili powder

cook's tip

Vary the vegetables used, or use those to hand. If preferred, use a few drops of chili sauce instead of chili powder, but remember it is very hot!

2

5

6

1 Using a sharp knife, cut the beef into thin strips and place them in a shallow glass bowl.

2 Add the garlic, scallions, soy sauce, and sesame oil and mix together well, turning the beef to coat. Cover and leave to marinate in the refrigerator for 30 minutes.

3 Cook the noodles in a pan of boiling water for 3–4 minutes. Drain the noodles thoroughly and set aside until required.

4 Put the beef stock in a large pan and bring to a boil.

5 Add the beef, together with the marinade, the corn, leek, and broccoli. Cover and leave to simmer over a low heat for 7–10 minutes, or until the beef and vegetables are tender and cooked through.

6 Stir in the noodles and chili powder and cook for a further 2–3 minutes. Transfer to bowls and serve immediately.

chili fish soup

Shiitake mushrooms add an intense flavor to this soup which is unique.
Try to obtain them if you can, otherwise use opencap mushrooms, sliced.

Serves 4

½ oz shiitake dried mushrooms

2 tbsp sunflower oil

1 onion, sliced

1½ cups snow peas

1½ cups bamboo shoots

3 tbsp sweet chili sauce

5 cups fish or vegetable stock

3 tbsp light soy sauce

2 tbsp fresh cilantro

1 lb cod fillet, skinned and cubed

variation

Cod is used in this recipe as it is a meaty white fish. For real luxury, use angler fish tail instead.

cook's tip

There are many different varieties of dried mushrooms, but shiitake are best. They are not cheap, but a small amount will go a long way.

1

3

4

1 Place the mushrooms in a large bowl. Pour over enough boiling water to cover and leave to stand for 5 minutes. Drain the mushrooms thoroughly. Using a sharp knife, roughly chop the mushrooms.

2 Heat the sunflower oil in a preheated wok. Add the onion to the wok and stir-fry for 5 minutes, or until softened.

3 Add the snow peas, bamboo shoots, chili sauce, stock, and soy sauce to the wok and bring to a boil.

4 Add the cilantro and cubed fish to the wok. Leave to simmer for 5 minutes or until the fish is cooked through.

5 Transfer the soup to warm bowls, garnish with extra cilantro if wished and serve hot.

italian fish soup

This colorful mixed seafood soup would be superbly complemented by
a dry white wine. It is an excellent soup for a special occasion.

1

3

Serves 4

4 tbsp butter

1 lb assorted fish fillets, such as red mullet
    and snapper

1 lb prepared seafood, such as squid
    and shrimp

8 oz fresh crabmeat

1 large onion, sliced

¼ cup all-purpose flour

5 cups fish stock

¾ cup dried pasta shapes, such as ditalini or
    elbow macaroni

1 tbsp anchovy extract

grated rind and juice of 1 orange

¼ cup dry sherry

1¼ cups heavy cream

salt and black pepper

crusty brown bread, to serve

5

1 Melt the butter in a large pan, add
the fish fillets, seafood, crabmeat,
and onion and cook gently over a low
heat for 6 minutes.

2 Add the flour to the mixture, stirring
thoroughly to avoid any lumps.

3 Gradually add the fish stock, stirring
constantly, until the soup comes to
a boil. Reduce the heat and simmer for
30 minutes.

4 Add the pasta to the pan and cook
for a further 10 minutes.

5 Stir in the anchovy extract, orange
rind, orange juice, sherry, and
heavy cream. Season to taste with salt
and pepper.

6 Heat the soup until completely
warmed through. Transfer the soup
to a tureen or to warm soup bowls and
serve with crusty brown bread.

mussel & potato soup

This quick and easy soup would make a delicious summer lunch served with fresh crusty bread. Make the most of mussels in season.

Serves 4

1 lb 10 oz mussels

2 tbsp olive oil

pepper

7 tbsp unsalted butter

2 slices rindless fatty bacon, chopped

1 onion, chopped

2 garlic cloves, finely chopped

½ cup all purpose flour

1 lb potatoes, thinly sliced

¼ cup dried conchigliette

1¼ cups heavy cream

1 tbsp lemon juice

salt and pepper

2 egg yolks

2 tbsp finely chopped fresh parsley and
    lemon wedges, to garnish

1 Debeard the mussels and scrub them under cold water for 5 minutes. Discard any mussels that do not close immediately when sharply tapped.

2 Bring a large pan of water to a boil, add the mussels, oil, and a little pepper and cook until the mussels open.

3 Drain the mussels, reserving the cooking liquid. Discard any mussels that are closed. Remove the mussels from their shells.

4 Melt the butter in a large pan, add the bacon, onion, and garlic and cook for 4 minutes. Carefully stir in the flour. Measure 5 cups of the reserved cooking liquid and stir it into the pan.

5 Add the potatoes to the pan and simmer for 5 minutes. Add the conchigliette and simmer for a further 10 minutes.

6 Add the cream and lemon juice, season to taste with salt and pepper, then add the mussels to the pan.

7 Blend the egg yolks with 1-2 tablespoons of the remaining cooking liquid, stir into the pan and cook for 4 minutes.

8 Ladle the soup into 4 warm individual soup bowls, garnish with the chopped fresh parsley and lemon wedges and serve immediately.

2

3

6

crab & ginger soup

Two classic ingredients in Chinese cooking are blended together
in this recipe for a special soup.

1

2

3

Serves 4

1 carrot, chopped

1 leek, chopped

1 bay leaf

3¾ cups fish stock

2 medium-sized cooked crabs

1-inch piece fresh gingerroot, grated

1 tsp light soy sauce

½ tsp ground star anise

salt and pepper

1 Put the carrot, leek, bay leaf, and stock into a large pan and bring to a boil. Reduce the heat, cover, and leave to simmer for about 10 minutes, or until the vegetables are nearly tender.

2 Meanwhile, remove all of the meat from the cooked crabs. Break off the claws, break the joints, and remove the meat (you may require a fork or skewer for this). Add the crabmeat to the saucepan of fish stock.

3 Add the gingerroot, soy sauce, and star anise to the fish stock and bring to a boil. Leave to simmer for about 10 minutes, or until the vegetables are tender and the crab is heated through. Season to taste with salt and pepper.

4 Ladle the soup into warmed serving bowls and garnish with crab claws. Serve at once.

cook's tip

If fresh crabmeat is unavailable, use drained canned crabmeat or thawed frozen crabmeat instead.

cook's tip

To prepare cooked crab, loosen the meat from the shell by banging the back of the underside with a clenched fist. Stand the crab on its edge with the shell towards you. Force the shell from the body with your thumbs. Twist off the legs and claws and remove the meat. Twist off the tail and discard. Remove and discard the gills from each side of the body. Cut the body in half along the center and remove all of the meat. Scoop the brown meat from the shell with a spoon.

coconut & crab soup

Thai red curry paste is quite fiery, but adds a superb flavor to this dish.
It is available in jars or packets from supermarkets.

2

3

4

Serves 4

1 tbsp peanut oil

2 tbsp Thai red curry paste

1 red bell pepper, seeded and sliced

2½ cups coconut milk

2½ cups fish stock (nam pla)

2 tbsp fish sauce

8 oz canned or fresh white crabmeat

8 oz fresh or frozen crab claws

2 tbsp chopped fresh cilantro

3 scallions, trimmed and sliced

1 Heat the oil in a large
preheated wok.

2 Add the red curry paste and red bell
pepper to the wok and stir-fry for
1 minute.

3 Add the coconut milk, fish stock,
and fish sauce to the wok and bring
to a boil.

4 Add the crabmeat, crab claws,
cilantro, and scallions to the wok.
Stir the mixture well and heat thoroughly
for 2–3 minutes.

5 Transfer the soup to warm bowls
and serve hot.

cook's tip

Coconut milk adds a sweet and
creamy flavor to the dish.
It is available in powdered
form or in tins ready to use.

cook's tip

Clean the wok after each
use by washing it with water,
using a mild detergent if
necessary, and a soft cloth
or brush. Do not scrub or use
any abrasive cleaner as this
will scratch the surface.
Dry thoroughly with paper
towels or over a low heat,
then wipe the surface all
over with a little oil.
This forms a sealing layer
to protect the surface of the
wok from moisture and prevents
it rusting.

seven-spice eggplant

This is a really simple dish which is perfect served with a chili dip.

Serves 4

1 lb eggplant, wiped

1 egg white

3½ tbsp cornstarch

1 tsp salt

1 tbsp Thai seven-spice seasoning

oil, for deep-frying

1 Using a sharp knife, slice
the eggplant into thin rings.

2 Place the egg white in a small bowl
and whip until light and foamy.

3 Mix together the cornstarch, salt,
and seven-spice powder on a large
plate.

4 Heat the oil for deep-frying in a
large wok.

1

3

cook's tip

The best oil to use for deep-frying is peanut oil which has a high smoke point and mild flavor, so it will neither burn or taint the food. About 1 pint oil is sufficient.

cook's tip

Thai seven-spice seasoning can be found in the spice racks of most large stores.

5 Dip each piece of eggplant into the
beaten egg white then coat in the
cornstarch and seven-spice mixture.

6 Deep-fry the eggplant slices, in
batches, for 5 minutes, or until pale
golden and crispy.

7 Transfer the eggplant to absorbent
paper towels and leave to drain.
Transfer to serving plates and serve hot.

5

chinese omelet

This is a fairly filling omelet, as it contains chicken and shrimp.

It is cooked as a whole omelet and then sliced for serving.

2

4

5

Serves 4

8 eggs

2 cups cooked chicken, shredded

12 jumbo shrimp, peeled and deveined

2 tbsp chopped chives

2 tsp light soy sauce

dash of chili sauce

2 tbsp vegetable oil

1 Lightly beat the eggs in a large mixing bowl.

2 Add the shredded chicken and jumbo shrimp to the eggs, mixing well.

3 Stir in the chopped chives, soy sauce, and chili sauce, mixing well.

4 Heat the oil in a large skillet over a medium heat and add the egg mixture, tilting the skillet to coat the base completely. Cook over a medium heat, gently stirring the omelet with a fork, until the surface is just set and the underside is a golden brown color.

5 When the omelet is set, slide it out of the skillet, with the aid of a spatula.

6 Cut the omelet into squares or slices to serve.

variation

You could add extra flavor to the omelet by stirring in 3 tbsp finely chopped fresh cilantro or 1 tsp sesame seeds with the chives in step 3.

cook's tip

Add English peas or other vegetables to the omelet and serve as a main course for 2 people.

carrot, fennel & potato medley

This is a colorful dish of shredded vegetables in a fresh garlic and honey dressing. It is delicious served with crusty bread to mop up the dressing.

Serves 4

2 tbsp olive oil

1 potato, cut into thin strips

1 fennel bulb, cut into thin strips

2 carrots, grated

1 red onion, cut into thin strips

DRESSING

3 tbsp olive oil

1 tbsp garlic-wine vinegar

1 garlic clove, finely chopped

1 tsp Dijon mustard

2 tsp clear honey

salt and pepper

chopped chives and fennel fronds,
    to garnish

1

2

3

1 Heat the olive oil in a skillet, add the potato and fennel slices and cook for 2–3 minutes until beginning to brown. Remove from the skillet with a draining spoon and drain on paper towels.

2 Arrange the carrot, red onion, potato, and fennel in separate piles on a serving plate.

3 Mix the dressing ingredients together and pour over the vegetables. Toss well and sprinkle with chopped chives and fennel fronds. Serve immediately or leave in the refrigerator until required.

cook's tip

Fennel is an aromatic plant which has a delicate, aniseed flavor. It can be eaten raw in salads, or boiled, braised, sautéed or broiled. For this salad, if fennel is unavailable, substitute 12 oz sliced leeks.

variation

Use mixed, grilled bell peppers or shredded leeks in this dish for variety, or add beansprouts and a segmented orange, if you prefer.

hummus & garlic toasts

Hummus is a real favorite spread on these garlic toasts for a
delicious appetizer or as part of a light lunch.

Serves 4

14 oz can garbanzo beans

juice of 1 large lemon

6 tbsp sesame seed paste

2 tbsp olive oil

2 garlic cloves, finely chopped

salt and pepper

1 ciabatta loaf, sliced

2 garlic cloves, finely chopped

1 tbsp chopped fresh cilantro

4 tbsp olive oil

chopped fresh cilantro and black olives,
    to garnish

2

3

5

cook's tip

Make the hummus 1 day in
advance, and chill, covered,
in the refrigerator until
required. Garnish and serve.

1 To make the hummus, firstly drain the garbanzo beans, reserving a little of the liquid. Put the garbanzo beans and liquid in a food processor and blend, gradually adding the reserved liquid and lemon juice. Blend well after each addition until smooth.

2 Stir in the sesame seed paste and all but 1 teaspoon of the olive oil. Add the garlic, season to taste, and blend again until smooth.

3 Spoon the hummus into a serving dish. Drizzle the remaining olive oil over the top, garnish with chopped cilantro and olives. Leave to chill in the refrigerator while preparing the toasts.

4 Lay the slices of ciabatta on a broiler rack in a single layer.

5 Mix the garlic, cilantro and olive oil together and drizzle over the bread slices. Cook under a hot broiler for 2–3 minutes until golden brown, turning once. Serve hot with the hummus.

crispy seaweed

This is a tasty Chinese appetizer or accompaniment which is not all that it seems. Pak choi is fried, salted, and tossed with pine nuts, seaweed being totally absent from the recipe!

Serves 4

2.4 lb pak choi

peanut oil, for deep frying (about 3¾ cups)

1 tsp salt

1 tbsp superfine sugar

2½ tbsp toasted pine nuts

1 Rinse the pak choi leaves under cold running water, then pat dry thoroughly with absorbent paper towels.

2 Roll up each pak choi leaf, then slice through thinly so that the leaves are finely shredded.

3 Heat the oil in a large wok. Carefully add the shredded leaves and fry for about 30 seconds or until they shrivel up and become crispy (you may need to do this in about 4 batches).

cook's tip

As a time-saver you can use a food processor to shred the pak choi finely. Make sure you use only the best leaves; sort through the pak choi and discard any tough, outer leaves as these will spoil the overall taste and texture of the dish.

1

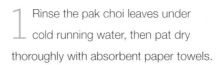

2

4

4 Remove the crispy seaweed from the wok with a draining spoon and drain on absorbent paper towels.

5 Transfer the crispy seaweed to a large bowl and toss with the salt, sugar, and pine nuts. Serve immediately.

variation

Use savoy cabbage instead of the pak choi if it is unavailable, making sure the leaves are well dried before frying.

paprika chips

These wafer-thin potato chips are great cooked over a grill and served with spicy chicken or pork. They also work well broiled, but they do not take on the 'smokey' flavor.

Serves 4

2 large potatoes

3 tbsp olive oil

½ tsp paprika pepper

salt

1

1 Using a sharp knife, slice the potatoes very thinly so that they are almost transparent. Drain the potato slices thoroughly and pat dry with paper towels.

2 Heat the oil in a large skillet and add the paprika, stirring constantly, to ensure that the paprika doesn't catch and burn.

3 Add the potato slices to the skillet and cook them in a single layer for about 5 minutes or until the potato slices just begin to curl slightly at the edges.

4 Remove the potato slices from the pan using a perforated spoon and transfer them to paper towels to drain thoroughly.

4

5

5 Thread the potato slices on to several wooden kabob skewers.

6 Sprinkle the potato slices with a little salt and cook over a medium hot grill or under a medium broiler for 10 minutes, turning frequently, until the potato slices begin to crisp. Sprinkle with a little more salt, if preferred, and serve.

variation

You could use curry powder or any other spice to flavor the chips instead of the paprika, if you prefer.

mixed bean pâté

This is a really quick appetizer to prepare if canned beans are used.

Choose a wide variety of beans for color and flavor or use a can of mixed beans.

Serves 4

14 oz can mixed beans, drained

2 tbsp olive oil

juice of 1 lemon

2 garlic cloves, finely chopped

1 tbsp chopped fresh cilantro

2 scallions, chopped

salt and pepper

shredded scallions, to garnish

cook's tip

Use canned beans which have no salt or sugar added and always rinse thoroughly before use.

cook's tip

Serve the pâté with warm pocket bread or granary toast.

1 Rinse the beans thoroughly under cold running water and drain well.

2 Transfer the beans to a food processor or blender and process until smooth. Alternatively, place the beans in a bowl and mash with a fork or potato masher.

3 Add the olive oil, lemon juice, garlic, cilantro, and scallions, and blend until fairly smooth. Season with salt and pepper to taste.

4 Transfer the pâté to a serving bowl and chill for at least 30 minutes. Garnish with shredded scallions and serve.

2

3

3

tuscan chicken livers on toast

Crostini are small pieces of toast with a savory topping.

In Italy this is a popular antipasto dish.

Serves 4

2 tbsp olive oil

1 garlic clove, finely chopped

8 oz fresh or frozen chicken livers

2 tbsp white wine

2 tbsp lemon juice

4 fresh sage leaves, finely chopped
    or 1 tsp dried, crumbled sage

salt and pepper

4 slices ciabatta or other Italian bread

wedges of lemon, to garnish

1

Heat the olive oil in a skillet and sauté the garlic for 1 minute.

2

Rinse and roughly chop the chicken livers, using a sharp knife.

3

Add the chicken livers to the skillet together with the white wine and lemon juice. Cook for 3–4 minutes or until the juices from the chicken liver run clear.

4

Stir in the sage and season to taste with salt and pepper.

5

Under a preheated broiler, toast the bread for 2 minutes on both sides or until golden-brown.

1

2

3

cook's tip

Overcooked liver is dry and tasteless. Cook the chopped liver for only 3-4 minutes — it should be soft and tender.

variation

Another way to make crostini is to slice a crusty loaf or a French loaf into small rounds or squares. Heat the olive oil in a skillet and sauté the slices of bread until golden brown and crisp on both sides. Remove the crostini from the pan with a draining spoon and leave to drain on paper towels. Top with the chicken livers.

6

Spoon the hot chicken livers on top of the toasted bread and serve garnished with a wedge of lemon.

chicken pan bagna

Perfect for a picnic or packed lunch, this Mediterranean-style sandwich can be prepared in advance.

5 Thinly slice the chicken and arrange on top of the bread. Arrange the tomatoes and drained anchovies on top of the chicken.

6 Scatter with the chopped black olives and plenty of black pepper. Sandwich the loaf back together and wrap tightly in foil until required. Cut into slices to serve.

Serves 6

1 large French stick

1 garlic clove

¼ cup olive oil

¼ oz canned anchovy fillets

2 oz cold roast chicken

2 large tomatoes, sliced

8 large, pitted black olives, chopped

pepper

1 Using a sharp bread knife, cut the French stick in half lengthways and open out.

2 Cut the garlic clove in half and rub over the bread.

3 Sprinkle the cut surface of the bread with the olive oil.

4 Drain the anchovies and set aside.

1

2

5

variation

You could use Italian ciabatta or olive-studded focaccia bread instead of the French stick, if you prefer. The last few years have seen a veritable interest in different breads and stores now stock a wide range from home and abroad.

cook's tip

Arrange a few fresh basil leaves in between the tomato slices to add a warm, spicy flavor. Use a good quality olive oil in this recipe for extra flavor.

fresh figs with prosciutto

This colorful fresh salad is delicious at any time of the year.

Serves 4

1¼ oz arugula

4 fresh figs

4 slices prosciutto

4 tbsp olive oil

1 tbsp fresh orange juice

1 tbsp clear honey

1 small red chilli

cook's tip

Chilies can burn the skin for several hours after chopping, so it is advisable to wear gloves when you are handling the very hot varieties.

cook's tip

Parma, in the Emilia-Romagna region of Italy, is famous for its ham, prosciutto di Parma, said to be the best in the world.

2

3

5

1 Tear the arugula into more manageable pieces and arrange on 4 serving plates.

2 Using a sharp knife, cut each of the figs into quarters and place them on top of the arugula leaves.

3 Using a sharp knife, cut the prosciutto into strips and scatter over the arugula and figs.

4 Place the oil, orange juice, and honey in a screw-top jar. Shake the jar until the mixture emulsifies and forms a thick dressing. Transfer to a bowl.

5 Using a sharp knife, dice the chili, remembering not to touch your face before you have washed your hands (see Cook's Tip, left). Add the chopped chili to the dressing and mix well.

6 Drizzle the dressing over the prosciutto, arugula, and figs, tossing to mix well. Serve at once.

cured meats with olives & tomatoes

This is a typical antipasto dish with the cold cured meats, stuffed olives, and fresh tomatoes, basil, and balsamic vinegar.

Serves 4

4 plum tomatoes

1 tbsp balsamic vinegar

salt and pepper

6 canned anchovy fillets, drained and rinsed

4½ oz green olives, pitted

2 tbsp capers, drained and rinsed

6 oz mixed, cured meats, sliced

8 fresh basil leaves

1 tbsp extra virgin olive oil

crusty bread, to serve

1 Using a sharp knife, cut the tomatoes into evenly sized slices. Sprinkle the tomato slices with the balsamic vinegar and a little salt and pepper to taste and set aside.

2 Chop the anchovy fillets into pieces measuring about the same length as the olives.

3 Push a piece of anchovy and a caper into each olive.

4 Arrange the sliced meat on 4 individual serving plates, together with the tomatoes, filled olives, and basil leaves.

5 Drizzle the olive oil over the sliced meat, tomatoes, and olives.

6 Serve the cured meats, olives, and tomatoes with lots of fresh crusty bread.

cook's tip

The cured meats for this recipe are up to your individual taste. They can include a selection of prosciutto, pancetta, bresaola (dried salt beef), and salame di Milano (pork and beef sausage).

cook's tip

Fill a screw-top jar with the stuffed olives, cover with olive oil, and use when required – they will keep for 1 month in the refrigerator.

1

2

4

deep-fried seafood

Deep-fried seafood is popular all around the Mediterranean, where fish of all kinds is fresh and abundant. Serve with garlic mayonnaise and lemon wedges.

Serves 4

7 oz prepared squid

7 oz raw jumbo shrimp, peeled

5¼ oz whitebait

oil, for deep-frying

2 tbsp all-purpose flour

salt and pepper

1 tsp dried basil

garlic mayonnaise (see Cook's Tip) and
    lemon wedges, to serve

2

cook's tip

To make garlic mayonnaise for serving with the deep-fried seafood, crush 2 garlic cloves, stir into 8 tbsp of mayonnaise and season with salt and pepper and a little chopped parsley.

1 Carefully rinse the squid, shrimp, and whitebait under cold running water, completely removing any dirt or grit.

2 Using a sharp knife, slice the squid into rings, leaving the tentacles whole.

3 Heat the oil in a large saucepan to 350°–375°F or until a cube of bread browns in 30 seconds.

4 Place the flour in a bowl and season with the salt, pepper, and basil.

5 Roll the squid, shrimp, and whitebait in the seasoned flour until coated all over. Carefully shake off any excess flour.

6 Cook the seafood in the heated oil in batches for 2–3 minutes or until crispy and golden all over. Remove all of the seafood with a draining spoon and leave to drain thoroughly on paper towels.

7 Transfer the deep-fried seafood to serving plates and serve with garlic mayonnaise and lemon wedges.

5

6

chinese shrimp & mushroom omelet

This is called Foo Yung in China and is a classic dish which may be flavored with any ingredients you have to hand. It is a quick and delicious omelet.

4

Serves 4

3 tbsp sunflower oil

2 leeks, trimmed and sliced

12 oz raw jumbo shrimp

4 tbsp cornstarch

1 tsp salt

6 oz mushrooms, sliced

1¼ cups beansprouts

6 eggs

deep-fried leeks, to garnish (optional)

5

6

1 Heat the sunflower oil in a preheated wok. Add the leeks and stir-fry for 3 minutes.

2 Rinse the shrimp under cold running water and then pat dry with absorbent paper towels.

3 Mix together the cornstarch and salt in a large bowl.

4 Add the shrimp to the cornstarch and salt mixture and toss to coat all over.

cook's tip

If liked, divide the mixture into 4 once the initial cooking has taken place in step 6 and cook 4 individual omelets.

5 Add the shrimp to the wok and stir-fry until the shrimp are almost cooked through.

6 Add the mushrooms and beansprouts to the wok and stir-fry for a further 2 minutes.

7 Beat the eggs with 3 tablespoons of cold water. Pour the egg mixture into the wok and cook until the egg sets, carefully turning over once. Turn out the omelet out on to a clean board, divide into 4 and serve hot, garnished with deep-fried leeks (if using).

salt & pepper shrimp

Szechuan peppercorns are very hot, adding heat and a red color to the shrimp. They are effectively offset by the sugar in this recipe.

Serves 4

2 tsp salt

1 tsp black pepper

2 tsp Szechuan peppercorns

1 tsp sugar

1 lb peeled raw jumbo shrimp

2 tbsp peanut oil

1 red chili, seeded and finely chopped

1 tsp freshly grated gingerroot

3 cloves garlic, finely chopped

scallions, sliced, to garnish

shrimp crackers, to serve

cook's tip

Szechuan peppercorns are also known as *farchiew*. These wild reddish-brown peppercorns from the Szechuan region of China add an aromatic flavor to a dish.

1

2

3

1 Grind the salt, black pepper and Szechuan peppercorns in a mortar and pestle. Mix the salt and pepper mixture with the sugar and set aside until required.

2 Rinse the shrimp under cold running water and pat dry with absorbent paper towels.

3 Heat the oil in a preheated wok. Add the shrimp, chili, gingerroot, and garlic, and stir-fry for 4–5 minutes, or until the shrimp are cooked through.

4 Add the salt and pepper mixture to the wok and stir-fry for 1 minute.

5 Transfer to warm serving bowls and garnish with the scallions. Serve hot with shrimp crackers.

cook's tip

Jumbo shrimps are widely available and are not only colorful and tasty, but they have a meaty texture, too. If cooked jumbo shrimp are used, add them with the salt and pepper mixture in step 4 — if the cooked shrimp are added any earlier they will toughen up and be inedible.

sesame shrimp toasts

These small toasts are easy to prepare and are one of the most popular Chinese appetizers in the West. Make sure you serve plenty of them as they are very tasty!

2

Serves 4

8 oz cooked, peeled shrimp

1 scallion

¼ tsp salt

1 tsp light soy sauce

1 tbsp cornstarch

1 egg white, beaten

3 thin slices white bread, crusts removed

4 tbsp sesame seeds

vegetable oil, for deep-frying

1 Put the shrimp and scallion in a food processor and process until finely ground. Alternatively, chop them very finely. Transfer to a bowl and stir in the salt, soy sauce, cornstarch, and egg white.

2

3

2 Spread the mixture on to one side of each slice of bread. Spread the sesame seeds on top of the mixture, pressing down well.

3 Cut each slice into four equal triangles or strips.

4 Heat the oil for deep-frying in a wok until almost smoking. Carefully place the triangles in the oil, coated side down, and cook for 2–3 minutes, until golden brown. Remove with a draining spoon and drain on paper towels. Serve hot.

cook's tip

If wished, you could add ¼ tsp very finely chopped fresh gingerroot and 1 tsp Chinese rice wine to the shrimp mixture at the end of step 1.

cook's tip

Deep-fry the triangles in two batches, keeping the first batch warm while you cook the second, to prevent them from sticking together and overcooking.

Too frequently, leaf vegetables are overcooked and limp, with all the goodness and flavor boiled out, while salads are often nothing more than a dismal leaf or two of pale green lettuce with a slice of tomato and a dry ring of onion. Make the most of the wonderful range of fresh produce that is available in our shops and markets.Steam broccoli and cabbage so that they are colorful and crunchy. Enjoy the wonderfully appetizing shades of orange and yellow bell peppers and the almost unbelievable purple-brown of eggplant. Try grating root vegetables – carrots and daikon – to add flavor and texture to garnishes and casseroles. Look

out for red and curly lettuces to bring excitement to an enticing summer salad. Use sweet baby tomatoes in salads and on skewers, and raid your garden and windowsill for sprigs of fresh mint and basil leaves for a tangy garnish.

light meals
salads

yellow bell pepper salad

A colorful combination of yellow bell peppers, red radishes, and celery combine to give a wonderfully crunchy texture and fresh taste.

Serves 4

4 strips lean bacon, chopped

2 yellow bell peppers

8 radishes, washed and trimmed

1 stalk celery, finely chopped

3 plum tomatoes, cut into wedges

3 tbsp olive oil

1 tbsp fresh thyme

salt and pepper

cook's tip

Pre-packaged diced bacon can be purchased from most stores, which helps to save on preparation time.

1

cook's tip

Tomatoes are actually berries and are related to potatoes. There are many different shapes and sizes of this versatile fruit. The one most used in Italian cooking is the plum tomato which is very flavorsome.

1 Dry fry the chopped bacon in a skillet for 4–5 minutes or until crispy. Remove the bacon from the skillet, set aside and leave to cool until required.

2 Using a sharp knife, halve and seed the bell peppers. Slice the bell peppers into long strips.

3 Using a sharp knife, halve the radishes and cut them into wedges.

4 Mix together the bell peppers, radishes, celery, and tomatoes and toss the mixture in the olive oil and fresh thyme. Season to taste with a little salt and pepper.

5 Transfer the salad to serving plates and garnish with the reserved crispy bacon.

2

3

cabbage & walnut stir-fry

This is a really quick, one-pan dish using white and red cabbage for color and flavor. Don't overcook or the texture will be spoiled.

Serves 4

350 g/12 oz white cabbage

12 oz red cabbage

4 tbsp peanut oil

1 tbsp walnut oil

2 garlic cloves, finely chopped

8 scallions, trimmed

8 oz firm bean curd, cubed

2 tbsp lemon juice

3½ oz walnut halves

2 tsp Dijon mustard

2 tsp poppy seeds

salt and pepper

1 Using a sharp knife, shred the white and red cabbages thinly.

2 Heat the peanut and walnut oils in a preheated wok. Add the garlic, cabbage, scallions, and bean curd, and cook for 5 minutes, stirring.

3 Add the lemon juice, walnuts, and mustard, season with salt and pepper and cook for a further 5 minutes or until the cabbage is tender.

4 Transfer the stir-fry to a warm serving bowl, sprinkle with poppy seeds and serve.

1

2

3

cook's tip

As well as adding protein, vitamins, and useful fats to the diet, nuts and seeds add flavor and texture to vegetarian meals. Keep a good supply of them in your cupboard as they can be used in a great variety of dishes – salads, bakes, stir-fries to name but a few.

variation

Sesame seeds could be used instead of the poppy seeds and drizzle 1 tsp of sesame oil over the dish just before serving, if you wish.

spaghetti with anchovy & pesto sauce

This is an ideal dish for cooks in a hurry and for those who do not have much time for shopping, as it is prepared in minutes from pantry ingredients.

Serves 4

3 fl oz olive oil

2 garlic cloves, finely chopped

2 oz can anchovy fillets, drained

1 lb dried spaghetti

2 oz pesto sauce (store bought)

2 tbsp finely chopped fresh oregano

pepper

1 cup grated Parmesan cheese,
    plus extra for serving (optional)

2 fresh oregano sprigs, to garnish

1 Reserve 1 tablespoon of the oil and heat the remainder in a small pan. Add the garlic and sauté for 3 minutes.

2 Lower the heat, stir in the anchovies and cook, stirring occasionally, until the anchovies have disintegrated.

3 Bring a large pan of lightly salted water to a boil. Add the spaghetti and the remaining olive oil and cook until just tender, but still firm to the bite.

4 Add the pesto sauce and chopped fresh oregano to the anchovy mixture and then season with black pepper to taste.

1

2

4

5 Drain the spaghetti, using a draining spoon, and transfer to a warm serving dish. Pour the pesto sauce over the spaghetti and then sprinkle over the grated Parmesan cheese.

6 Garnish with oregano sprigs and serve with extra cheese, if using.

cook's tip

If you find canned anchovies much too salty, soak them in a saucer of cold milk for 5 minutes, drain and pat dry with kitchen towels before using.

variation

For a vegetarian alternative of this recipe, simply substitute drained sun-dried tomatoes for the anchovy fillets.

sweet potato & nut salad

Pecan nuts with their slightly bitter flavor are mixed with sweet potatoes in this recipe to make a sweet and sour salad with an interesting texture.

2

3

Serves 4

1 lb sweet potatoes, diced

2 celery stalks, sliced

4½ oz celery root, grated

2 scallions, sliced

1¼ oz pecan nuts, chopped

2 heads endive, separated

1 tsp lemon juice

thyme sprigs, to garnish

DRESSING

4 tbsp vegetable oil

1 tbsp garlic wine vinegar

1 tsp soft light brown sugar

2 tsp chopped fresh thyme

cook's tip

Sweet potatoes do not store as well as ordinary potatoes. It is best to store them in a cool, dark place (not the refrigerator) and use within 1 week of purchase.

6

1 Cook the sweet potatoes in a pan of boiling water for 5 minutes until tender. Drain thoroughly and leave to cool.

2 When cooled, stir in the celery stalks, celery root, scallions, and pecan nuts.

3 Line a salad plate with the endive leaves and sprinkle with lemon juice.

4 Spoon the potato mixture into the center of the leaves.

5 In a small bowl, whisk the dressing ingredients together.

6 Pour the dressing over the salad and serve at once, garnished with thyme sprigs.

variation

For variety, replace the garlic wine vinegar in the dressing with a different flavored oil, such as chili or herb.

scrambled bean curd on toast

This is a delicious dish which would also serve as a light lunch or supper.

Serves 4

6 tbsp margarine

1 lb marinated, firm bean curd

1 red onion, chopped

1 red bell pepper, chopped

4 ciabatta rolls

2 tbsp chopped mixed herbs

salt and pepper

fresh herbs, to garnish

1

2

4

cook's tip

Marinated bean curd adds extra flavor to this dish. Smoked bean curd could be used in its place.

cook's tip

Rub the cut surface of a garlic clove over the toasted ciabatta rolls for extra flavor.

1 Melt the margarine in a skillet and crumble the bean curd into the pan.

2 Add the chopped onion and bell pepper and cook for 3–4 minutes, stirring occasionally.

3 Meanwhile, slice the ciabatta rolls in half and toast under a hot broiler for about 2–3 minutes, turning once. Remove the toasts and transfer to a serving plate.

4 Add the herbs to the bean curd mixture, combine, and season.

5 Spoon the bean curd mixture on to the toast and garnish with fresh herbs. Serve at once.

potato, bell pepper, & mushroom hash

This is a quick one-pan dish which is ideal for a quick snack. Packed with color and flavor it is very versatile and you can add any other vegetable you have at hand.

Serves 4

1½ lb potatoes, cubed

1 tbsp olive oil

2 garlic cloves, finely chopped

1 green bell pepper, cubed

1 yellow bell pepper, cubed

3 tomatoes, diced

1 cup white mushrooms, halved

1 tbsp Worcestershire sauce

2 tbsp chopped basil

salt and pepper

fresh basil sprigs, to garnish

warm, crusty bread, to serve

4

2

5

cook's tip

Most brands of Worcestershire sauce contain anchovies, but vegetarian varieties are available, if preferred.

1 Cook the potatoes in a saucepan of boiling salted water for 7–8 minutes. Drain well and reserve.

2 Heat the oil in a large, heavy-bottomed skillet and cook the potatoes for 8–10 minutes, stirring until browned.

3 Add the garlic and bell peppers and cook for 2–3 minutes.

4 Stir in the tomatoes and mushrooms and cook, stirring, for 5–6 minutes.

5 Stir in the Worcestershire sauce and basil and season well. Garnish with basil and serve with crusty bread.

variation

This dish can also be eaten cold as a salad.

marinated broiled fennel

Fennel has a wonderful aniseed flavor which is ideal for broiling or grilling. Marinated in lime, garlic, oil, and mustard, this recipe is really delicious.

1

2

Serves 4

2 fennel bulbs

1 red bell pepper, cut into large cubes

1 lime, cut into eight wedges

2 tbsp lime juice

4 tbsp olive oil

2 garlic cloves, finely chopped

1 tsp whole-grain mustard

1 tbsp chopped thyme

fennel fronds, to garnish

crisp salad, to serve

1 Cut each of the fennel bulbs into eight pieces and place in a shallow dish. Mix in the bell pepper.

2 To make the marinade, combine the lime juice, oil, garlic, mustard, and

thyme. Pour the marinade over the fennel and bell peppers and leave to marinate for 1 hour.

3 Thread the fennel and bell peppers on to wooden skewers with the lime wedges. Preheat a broiler to medium and broil the kabobs for 10 minutes, turning and basting with the marinade.

4 Transfer to serving plates, garnish with fennel fronds and serve with a crisp salad.

3

cook's tip

Soak the skewers in water for 20 minutes before using to prevent them from burning during cooking.

variation

Substitute 2 tbsp orange juice for the lime juice and add 1 tbsp honey, if you prefer.

tagliarini with gorgonzola

This simple, creamy pasta sauce is a classic Italian recipe.

1

Serves 4

2 tbsp butter

8 oz Gorgonzola cheese, roughly crumbled

¾ cup heavy cream

2 tbsp dry white wine

1 tsp cornstarch

4 fresh sage sprigs, finely chopped

salt and white pepper

14 oz dried tagliarini

2 tbsp olive oil

cook's tip

Gorgonzola is one of the world's oldest veined cheeses and, arguably, its finest. When buying, always check that it is creamy yellow with delicate green veining. Avoid hard or discolored cheese. It should have a rich, piquant aroma, not a bitter smell. If you find Gorgonzola too strong or rich, you could substitute Danish blue.

1 Melt the butter in a heavy-bottomed pan. Stir in 6 oz of the Gorgonzola cheese and melt, over a low heat, for about 2 minutes.

2 Add the cream, wine, and cornstarch and beat with a whisk until fully incorporated.

3 Stir in the sage and season to taste with salt and white pepper. Bring to a boil over a low heat, whisking constantly, until the sauce thickens. Remove from the heat and set aside while you cook the pasta.

4 Bring a large pan of lightly salted water to a boil. Add the tagliarini and 1 tablespoon of the olive oil. Cook the pasta for 12–14 minutes or until just tender, drain thoroughly, and toss in the remaining olive oil. Transfer the pasta to a serving dish and keep warm.

5 Return the saucepan containing the sauce to a low heat to reheat the sauce, whisking constantly. Spoon the Gorgonzola sauce over the tagliarini, generously sprinkle over the remaining cheese and serve immediately.

2

3

mixed bean pan-fry

Fresh green beans have a wonderful flavor that is hard to beat.
If you cannot find fresh beans, use thawed, frozen beans instead.

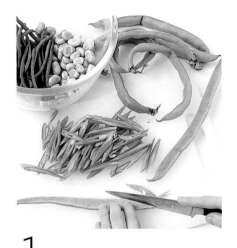

1

variation

Use smoked bean curd instead
of marinated bean curd for an
alternative flavor.

variation

Add lime juice instead of
lemon, for an alternative
citrus flavor.

Serves 4

4 cups mixed green beans, such as
    fava beans or dwarf beans

2 tbsp vegetable oil

2 garlic cloves, finely chopped

1 red onion, halved and sliced

8 oz firm marinated bean curd, diced

1 tbsp lemon juice

½ tsp turmeric

1 tsp ground mixed spice

½ cup vegetable stock

2 tsp sesame seeds

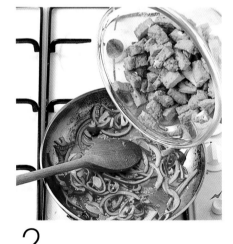

2

1 Trim and chop the green beans
shell the fava beans, and set aside
until required.

2 Heat the oil in a skillet and sauté
the garlic and onion for 2 minutes,
stirring well.

3 Add the bean curd and cook for
2–3 minutes until just beginning
to brown.

4 Add the green beans and fava
beans. Stir in the lemon juice,
turmeric, mixed spice, and vegetable
stock and bring to a boil.

5 Reduce the heat and simmer for
5–7 minutes or until the beans are
tender. Sprinkle with sesame seeds and
serve immediately.

4

beet & orange rice salad

You must use freshly cooked beet in this unusual combination of colors and flavors. Beet that has been soaked in vinegar will spoil the delicate balance.

Serves 4

1½ cups long-grain and wild rices
  (see Cook's Tip, below)
4 large oranges
1 lb cooked beet, peeled
salt and pepper
2 heads of endive
fresh snipped chives, to garnish

DRESSING
4 tbsp low-fat unsweetened yogurt
1 garlic clove, finely chopped
1 tbsp whole-grain mustard
½ tsp finely grated orange rind
2 tsp clear honey

1 Cook the rices according to the directions on the packet. Drain and set aside to cool.

2 Meanwhile, slice the top and bottom off each orange. Using a sharp knife, remove the skin and pith. Holding the orange over a bowl to catch the juice, carefully slice between each segment. Place the segments in a separate bowl. Cover the juice and leave to chill in the refrigerator until required.

3 Drain the beet if necessary and dice into cubes. Mix with the orange segments, cover, and leave to chill.

4 When the rice has cooled, mix in the reserved orange juice and season with salt and pepper to taste.

5 Line 4 serving bowls or plates with the endive leaves. Spoon over the rice and top with the beet and orange segments.

6 Mix all the dressing ingredients together and spoon over the salad, or serve separately in a bowl, if preferred. Garnish with fresh snipped chives.

cook's tip

Look out for boxes of ready-mixed long-grain and wild rices. Alternatively, cook 1 cup white rice and ¹/₄ cup wild rice separately.

2

3

5

tagliatelle with zucchini sauce

This is a really fresh tasting dish which is ideal with a crisp white wine and some crusty bread for a light summer's day lunch.

Serves 4

1 lb 7 oz zucchini

6 tbsp olive oil

3 garlic cloves, finely chopped

3 tbsp chopped basil

2 red chiles, sliced

juice of 1 large lemon

5 tbsp light cream

4 tbsp grated Parmesan cheese

salt and pepper

8 oz tagliatelle

1

1 Using a vegetable peeler, slice the zucchini into ribbons.

2 Heat the oil in a skillet and sauté the garlic for 30 seconds.

3 Add the zucchini and cook over a gentle heat, stirring, for 5–7 minutes.

4 Stir in the basil, chiles, lemon juice, light cream, and grated Parmesan cheese, and season with salt and pepper to taste.

5 Meanwhile, cook the tagliatelle in a large pan of lightly salted boiling water for 10 minutes until 'al dente'. Drain the pasta thoroughly and put in a warm serving bowl.

6 Pile the zucchini mixture on top of the pasta. Serve immediately.

3

4

variation

Lime juice and zest could be used instead of the lemon as an alternative.

refried beans with tortillas

Refried beans are a classic Mexican dish and are usually served as an
accompaniment. They are, however, delicious when served with warm tortillas
and a quick onion relish.

Serves 4

2 tbsp olive oil

1 onion, finely chopped

3 garlic cloves, finely chopped

1 green chile, chopped

14 oz can red kidney beans, drained

14 oz can pinto beans, drained

2 tbsp chopped cilantro

¼ cup vegetable stock

8 wheat tortillas

¼ cup Cheddar cheese, grated

salt and pepper

RELISH

4 scallions, chopped

1 red onion, chopped

1 green chile, chopped

1 tbsp garlic-wine vinegar

1 tsp superfine sugar

1 tomato, chopped

2

3

5

4 Place the tortillas on a baking sheet
and heat through in a warm oven
for 1–2 minutes.

5 Mix together the
relish ingredients.

6 Spoon the beans into a serving dish
and top with the cheese. Season
well. Roll the tortillas and serve with the
relish and beans.

1 Heat the oil in a large skillet.
Add the onion and sauté for 3–5
minutes. Add the garlic and chile and
cook for 1 minute.

2 Mash the beans with a potato
masher and stir into the pan with
the cilantro.

3 Stir in the stock and cook the
beans, stirring, for 5 minutes until
soft and pulpy.

cook's tip

Add a little more liquid
to the beans when they are
cooking if they begin to catch
on the bottom of the skillet.

potato, radish, & cucumber salad

The radishes and the herb and mustard dressing give this colorful salad a mild mustard flavor which complements the potatoes perfectly.

Serves 4

1 lb new potatoes, scrubbed and halved

½ cucumber, sliced thinly

2 tsp salt

1 bunch radishes, sliced thinly

DRESSING

1 tbsp Dijon mustard

2 tbsp olive oil

1 tbsp white wine vinegar

2 tbsp mixed chopped herbs

1 Cook the potatoes in a pan of boiling water for 10-15 minutes or until tender. Drain and leave to cool.

2 Meanwhile spread out the cucumber slices on a plate and sprinkle with the salt. Leave to stand for 30 minutes, then rinse under cold running water and pat dry with paper towels.

3 Arrange the cucumber and radish slices on a serving plate in a decorative pattern and pile the cooked potatoes in the center of the slices.

4 In a small bowl, mix the dressing ingredients together. Pour the dressing over the salad, tossing well to coat all of the salad ingredients. Leave to chill in the refrigerator before serving.

variation

Dijon mustard has a mild clean taste which is perfect for this salad as it does not overpower the other flavors. If unavailable, use another mild mustard — English mustard is too strong for this salad.

2

2

3

cook's tip

The cucumber adds not only color but a real freshness to the salad. It is salted and left to stand to remove the excess water which would make the salad soggy. Wash the cucumber well to remove all of the salt, before adding to the salad.

vegetable spaghetti with lemon dressing

Steaming vegetables helps to preserve their nutritional content and allows them to retain their bright, natural colors, and crunchy texture.

Serves 4

8 oz celery root

2 medium carrots

2 medium leeks

1 small red bell pepper

1 small yellow bell pepper

2 garlic cloves

1 tsp celery seeds

1 tbsp lemon juice

10½ oz spaghetti

celery leaves, chopped, to garnish

LEMON DRESSING

1 tsp finely grated lemon rind

1 tbsp lemon juice

4 tbsp low-fat unsweetened yogurt

salt and pepper

2 tbsp snipped fresh chives

1

2

4

5 When the spaghetti and vegetables are cooked, mix the ingredients for the lemon dressing together.

6 Transfer the spaghetti and vegetables into a warm serving bowl and mix with the dressing. Garnish with chopped celery leaves and serve.

1 Peel the celery root and carrots, cut into thin matchsticks and place in a bowl. Trim and slice the leeks, rinse under running water to flush out any trapped dirt, then shred finely. Halve, seed, and slice the bell peppers. Peel and thinly slice the garlic. Add all of the vegetables to the bowl with the celery root and the carrots.

2 Toss the vegetables with the celery seeds and lemon juice.

3 Bring a large pan of water to a boil and cook the spaghetti according to the directions on the packet. Drain and keep warm.

4 Meanwhile, bring another large pan of water to a boil, put the vegetables in a steamer or strainer and place over the boiling water. Cover and steam for 6–7 minutes or until just tender.

olive, bell pepper & cherry tomato pasta

The sweet cherry tomatoes in this recipe add color and flavor and are complemented by the black olives and bell peppers.

Serves 4

2 cups penne

2 tbsp olive oil

2 tbsp butter

2 garlic cloves, minced

1 green bell pepper, thinly sliced

1 yellow bell pepper, thinly sliced

16 cherry tomatoes, halved

1 tbsp chopped oregano

½ cup dry white wine

2 tbsp quartered, pitted black olives

2¾ oz arugula

salt and pepper

fresh oregano sprigs, to garnish

1 Cook the pasta in a pan of boiling salted water for 8–10 minutes or until 'al dente'. Drain thoroughly.

2 Heat the oil and butter in a pan until the butter melts. Sauté the garlic for 30 seconds. Add the bell peppers and cook for 3–4 minutes, stirring.

3 Stir in the cherry tomatoes, oregano, wine, and olives and cook for 3–4 minutes. Season well with salt and pepper and stir in the arugula until just wilted.

4 Transfer the pasta to a serving dish, spoon over the sauce, and mix well. Garnish and serve.

variation

If arugula is unavailable, spinach makes a good substitute. Follow the same cooking directions as for arugula.

2

3

3

cook's tip

Ensure that the pan is large enough to prevent the pasta from sticking together during cooking.

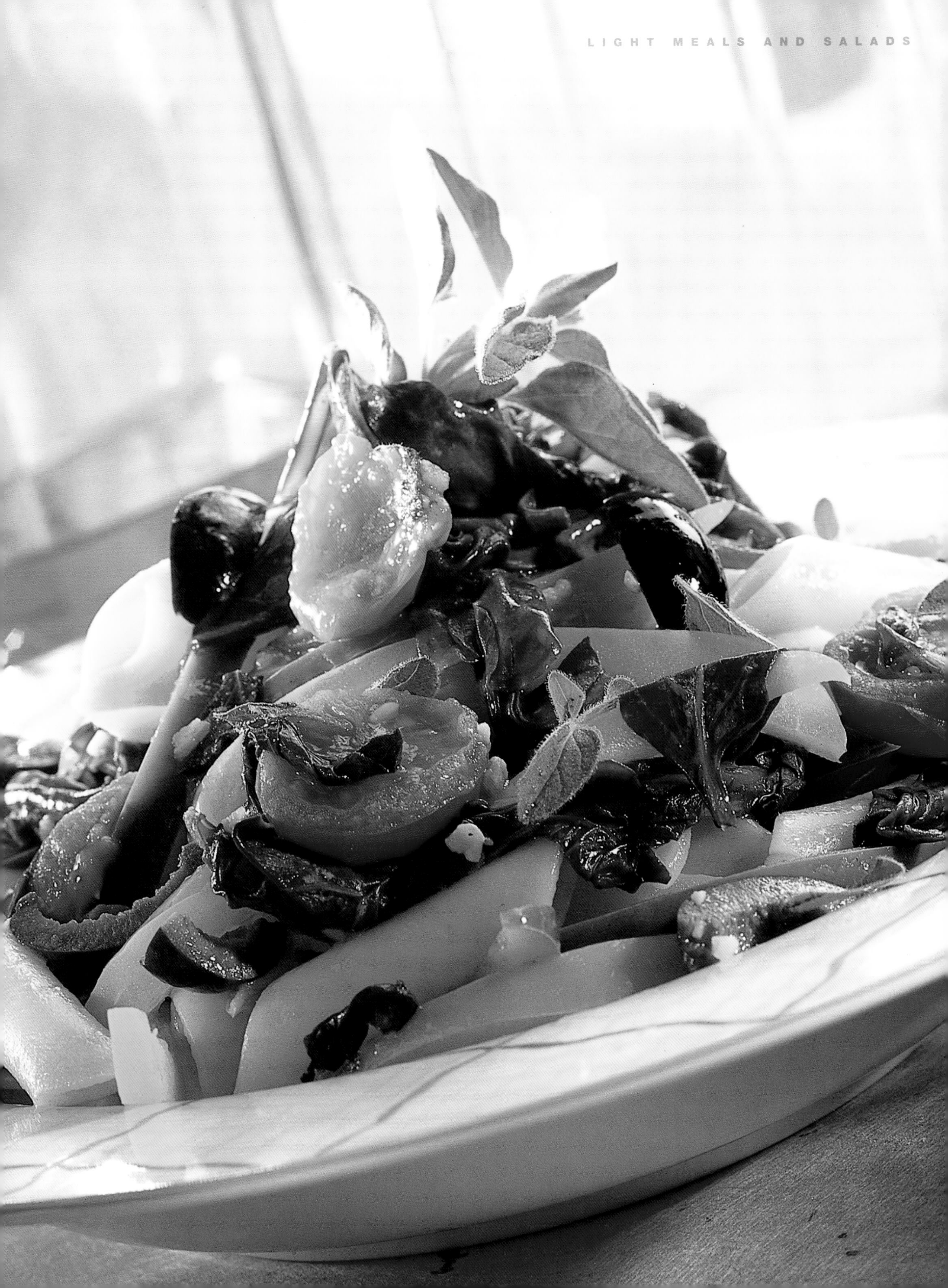

garlic mushrooms on toast

This is so simple to prepare and looks great if you use a variety of mushrooms for shape and texture. Cooked in garlic butter, they are simply irresistible.

Serves 4

6 tbsp margarine

2 garlic cloves, finely chopped

4 cups mixed mushrooms, such as open-
   cap, button, oyster, and shiitake, sliced

8 slices French bread

1 tbsp chopped parsley

salt and pepper

2

3

cook's tip

Store mushrooms for 24-36 hours in the refrigerator, in paper bags, as they sweat in plastic. Wild mushrooms should be washed but other varieties can simply be wiped with a paper towel.

cook's tip

Add seasonings, such as curry powder or chili powder, to the mushrooms for extra flavor, if liked.

1 Melt the margarine in a skillet. Add the garlic and sauté for 30 seconds, stirring.

2 Add the mushrooms and cook for 5 minutes, turning occasionally.

3 Toast the French bread slices under a preheated medium broiler for 2–3 minutes, turning once.

4 Transfer the toasts to a serving plate.

5 Toss the parsley into the mushrooms, mixing well, and season well with salt and pepper to taste.

6 Spoon the mushroom mixture over the bread and serve immediately.

5

spinach & pine nut pasta

Use any pasta shapes that you have for this recipe. Tricolore pasta represents the Italian flag and is visually the best to use.

2

Serves 4

8 oz pasta shapes or spaghetti

½ cup olive oil

2 garlic cloves, finely chopped

1 onion, quartered and sliced

3 large flat mushrooms, sliced

8 oz spinach

2 tbsp pine nuts

6 tbsp dry white wine

salt and pepper

Parmesan shavings, to garnish

cook's tip

'Al dente' means that the pasta should be tender but still have a bite to it.

cook's tip

Freshly grate a little nutmeg over the dish for extra flavor, as it is particularly good with spinach.

1 Cook the pasta in a pan of boiling salted water for 8–10 minutes or until 'al dente'. Drain well.

2 Meanwhile, heat the oil in a large skillet and sauté the garlic and onion for 1 minute.

3 Add the sliced mushrooms to the skillet and cook for 2 minutes, stirring occasionally.

4 Add the spinach and cook for 4–5 minutes or until the spinach has wilted.

5 Stir in the pine nuts and wine, season well, and cook for 1 minute.

6 Transfer the pasta to a warm serving bowl and toss the sauce into it, mixing well. Garnish with shavings of Parmesan cheese and serve.

3

5

pasta provençale

A combination of vegetables tossed in a tomato dressing, served on a bed of assorted salad leaves, makes a tasty main meal or an appetizing side dish.

Serves 4

8 oz penne

1 tbsp olive oil

salt and pepper

1 oz pitted black olive, drained and chopped

1 oz dry-pack sun-dried tomatoes, soaked, drained and chopped

14 oz can artichoke hearts, drained and halved

4 oz baby zucchini, trimmed and sliced

4 oz baby plum tomatoes, halved

3½ oz assorted baby salad leaves

shredded basil leaves, to garnish

DRESSING

4 tbsp sieved tomatoes

2 tbsp low-fat unsweetened yogurt

1 tbsp unsweetened orange juice

1 small bunch fresh basil, shredded

1

2

3

1 Cook the penne according to the directions on the packet. Do not overcook the pasta – it should still have 'bite'. Drain well and return to the pan. Stir in the olive oil, salt and pepper, olives, and sun-dried tomatoes. Leave to cool.

2 Gently mix the artichokes, zucchini, and plum tomatoes into the cooked pasta. Arrange the salad leaves in a serving bowl.

3 To make the dressing, mix all the ingredients together and toss into the vegetables and pasta.

4 Spoon the mixture on top of the salad leaves and garnish with shredded basil leaves.

variation

For a non-vegetarian version, stir 8 oz canned tuna in brine, drained, and flaked, into the pasta together with the vegetables. Other pasta shapes can be included — look out for farfalle and rotelle.

root vegetable salad

This colorful salad of grated vegetables is perfect for a light starter.
The peppery flavors of the daikon and radishes are refreshingly pungent.
Serve with some toasted bread and assorted salad leaves.

Serves 4

12 oz carrots

8 oz daikon

4 oz radishes

12 oz celery root

1 tbsp orange juice

2 stalks celery with leaves, washed
   and trimmed

3½ oz assorted salad leaves

1 oz walnut pieces

DRESSING

1 tbsp walnut oil

1 tbsp white wine vinegar

1 tsp whole-grain mustard

½ tsp finely grated orange rind

1 tsp celery seeds

salt and pepper

1 Peel and coarsely grate or very finely
  shred the carrots, daikon, and
radishes. Set aside in separate bowls.

2 Peel and coarsely grate or finely
  shred the celery root and mix with
the orange juice.

3 Remove the celery leaves and
  reserve. Finely chop the celery
stalks.

4 Divide the salad leaves among
  4 serving plates and arrange the
vegetables in small piles on top. Set
aside while you make the dressing.

5 Mix all of the dressing ingredients
  together and season well. Drizzle a
little over each salad. Shred the
reserved celery leaves and sprinkle over
the salad with the walnut pieces.

5

1

3

cook's tip

Also known as Chinese white
radish and mooli, daikon
resembles a large white
parsnip. It has crisp, slightly
pungent flesh, which can be
eaten raw or cooked. It is
a useful ingredient in
stir-fries. Fresh daikon tends
to have a stronger flavor than
store-bought.

mexican-style pizzas

Ready-made pizza bases are topped with a chili-flavored tomato sauce and topped with kidney beans, cheese, and jalapeño chiles in this blend of American, Italian, and Mexican cooking.

Serves 4

4 ready-made individual pizza bases

1 tbsp olive oil

7 oz can chopped tomatoes with garlic
    and herbs

2 tbsp tomato paste

7 oz can red kidney beans, drained
    and rinsed

4 oz corn nuts, thawed if frozen

1–2 tsp chili sauce

salt and pepper

1 large red onion, shredded

3½ oz reduced-fat Cheddar
    cheese, grated

1 large green chile, sliced into rings

2 tbsp fresh cilantro, chopped

cook's tip

For a low-fat Mexican-style
salad to serve with this pizza,
arrange sliced tomatoes, fresh
cilantro leaves and a few
slices of a small, ripe
avocado. Sprinkle with fresh
lime juice and coarse sea salt.
Avocados have quite a high oil
content, so eat in moderation.

1

3

3

1 Preheat the oven to 425°F. Arrange
the pizza bases on a cookie sheet
and brush them lightly with the oil.

2 In a bowl, mix together the chopped
tomatoes, tomato paste, kidney
beans, and corn, and add chili sauce to
taste. Season with salt and pepper.

3 Spread the tomato and kidney bean
mixture evenly over each pizza base
to cover. Top each pizza with shredded
onion and sprinkle with some grated
cheese and a few slices of green chile
to taste. Bake in the oven for about
20 minutes until the vegetables are
tender, the cheese has melted and the
base is crisp and golden.

4 Remove the pizzas from the cookie
sheet and transfer to serving plates.
Sprinkle with chopped cilantro and serve
immediately.

spaghetti with ricotta cheese

This light pasta dish has a delicate flavor ideally suited to a summer lunch.

Serves 4

12 oz dried spaghetti

3 tbsp olive oil

3 tbsp butter

2 tbsp chopped fresh flat leaf parsley

1 cup freshly ground almonds

½ cup ricotta cheese

pinch of grated nutmeg

pinch of ground cinnamon

¾ cup unsweetened yogurt

4 fl oz hot chicken stock

1 tbsp pine nuts

salt and pepper

fresh flat leaf parsley sprigs, to garnish

1 Bring a large pan of lightly salted water to a boil. Add the spaghetti and 1 tbsp of the oil and cook until tender, but still firm to the bite.

2 Drain the pasta, return to the pan, and toss with the butter and chopped parsley. Set aside and keep warm.

3 To make the sauce, mix together the ground almonds, ricotta cheese, nutmeg, cinnamon, and unsweetened yogurt over a low heat to form a thick paste. Gradually stir in the remaining oil. When the oil has been fully incorporated, gradually stir in the hot chicken stock, until smooth. Season to taste.

4 Transfer the spaghetti to a warm serving dish, pour over the sauce and toss together well (see Cook's Tip, below). Sprinkle over the pine nuts, garnish with the flat leaf parsley, and serve warm.

2

3

cook's tip

Use two large forks to toss spaghetti or other long pasta, so that it is thoroughly coated with the sauce. Special spaghetti forks are available from some cookware departments and kitchen stores. Holding one fork in each hand, gently ease the prongs under the pasta on each side and lift them towards the center. Continue this evenly and rhythmically until the pasta is completely coated.

3

potato, arugula & apple salad

This green and white salad is made with creamy, salty goat cheese.
Its distinctive flavor is perfect with salad greens.

Serves 4

2 large potatoes, unpeeled and sliced

2 green dessert apples, diced

1 tsp lemon juice

1 oz walnut pieces

4½ oz goat cheese, cubed

5½ oz arugula leaves

salt and pepper

DRESSING

2 tbsp olive oil

1 tbsp red wine vinegar

1 tsp clear honey

1 tsp fennel seeds

2

3

4

1 Cook the potatoes in a pan of boiling water for 15 minutes until tender. Drain and leave to cool. Transfer the cooled potatoes to a serving bowl.

2 Toss the diced apples in the lemon juice, drain and stir into the cold potatoes.

3 Add the walnut pieces, cheese cubes, and arugula leaves, then toss the salad to mix.

4 In a small bowl, whisk the dressing ingredients together and pour the dressing over the salad. Serve immediately.

cook's tip

Serve this salad immediately to prevent the apple from discoloring. Alternatively, prepare all of the other ingredients in advance and add the apple at the last minute.

variation

Use smoked or blue cheese instead of goat cheese, if you prefer. In addition, if arugula is unavailable use baby spinach instead.

pasta niçoise salad

Based on the classic French salad niçoise, this recipe contains pasta instead of potatoes. The very light olive oil dressing has the tang of capers and the fragrance of fresh basil.

2

Serves 4

8 oz farfalle

6 oz green beans, topped and tailed

12 oz fresh tuna steaks

salt and pepper

4 oz baby plum tomatoes, halved

8 anchovy fillets, drained on absorbent
    paper towels

2 tbsp capers in brine, drained

1 oz pitted black olives in brine, drained

fresh basil leaves, to garnish

DRESSING

1 tbsp olive oil

1 garlic clove, finely chopped

1 tbsp lemon juice

½ tsp finely grated lemon rind

1 tbsp shredded fresh basil leaves

3

1 Cook the pasta in lightly salted boiling water according to the directions on the packet until just cooked. Drain well, set aside and keep warm.

2 Bring a small pan of lightly salted water to a boil and cook the green beans for 5–6 minutes until just tender. Drain well and toss into the pasta. Set aside and keep warm.

3 Preheat the broiler to medium. Rinse and pat the tuna steaks dry on absorbent paper towels. Season on both sides with black pepper. Place the tuna steaks on the broiler rack and cook for 4–5 minutes on each side until cooked through.

4 Drain the tuna on absorbent paper towels and flake into bite-sized pieces. Toss the tuna into the pasta along with the tomatoes, anchovies, capers, and olives. Set aside and keep warm.

5 Meanwhile, prepare the dressing. Mix all the ingredients together and season well. Pour the dressing over the pasta mixture and mix carefully. Transfer to a warmed serving bowl and serve.

4

minted fennel salad

This is a very refreshing salad. The subtle liquorice flavor of fennel combines well with the cucumber and mint.

Serves 4

1 bulb fennel

lemon juice

2 small oranges

1 small or ½ a large cucumber

1 tbsp chopped mint

1 tbsp virgin olive oil

2 eggs, hard cooked

1

2

3

1 Using a sharp knife, trim the outer leaves from the fennel. Slice the fennel bulb thinly into a bowl of water and sprinkle with lemon juice (see Cook's Tip).

2 Grate the rind of the oranges over a bowl. Using a sharp knife, pare away the orange peel, then segment the orange by carefully slicing between each line of pith. Do this over the bowl in order to retain the juice.

3 Cut the cucumber into ½ inch rounds, and cut these into quarters. Add the cucumber and mint to the fennel and orange mixture.

4 Pour the olive oil over the fennel and cucumber salad and toss well.

5 Peel and quarter the eggs and use these to decorate the top of the salad. Serve at once.

cook's tip

Fennel will discolor if it is left for any length of time without a dressing. To prevent any discoloration, place it in a bowl of water and sprinkle with lemon juice.

cook's tip

Virgin olive oil, which has a fine aroma and flavor, is made by the cold pressing of olives. However, it may have a slightly higher acidity level than extra virgin oil.

potato & mixed vegetable salad with lemon mayonnaise

This salad is a medley of crunchy vegetables, mixed with sliced cooked potatoes and ham, then coated in a fresh-tasting lemon mayonnaise.

Serves 4

1 lb waxy new potatoes, scrubbed

1 carrot, cut into matchsticks

8 oz cauliflower flowerets

8 oz baby corn, halved lengthways

6 oz dwarf beans

6 oz ham, diced

1¼ oz mushrooms, sliced

salt and pepper

DRESSING

2 tbsp chopped fresh parsley

½ cup mayonnaise

½ cup natural yogurt

4 tsp lemon juice

rind of 1 lemon

2 tsp fennel seeds

1

2

1 Cook the potatoes in a pan of boiling water for 15 minutes or until tender. Drain and leave to cool. When the potatoes are cold, slice them thinly.

2 Meanwhile, cook the carrot matchsticks, cauliflower flowerets, baby corn, and dwarf beans in a pan of boiling water for 5 minutes. Drain well and leave to cool.

3 Reserve 1 tsp of the chopped parsley for the garnish. In a bowl, mix the remaining dressing ingredients together.

4

4 Arrange the vegetables on a salad platter and top with the ham strips and sliced mushrooms.

5 Spoon the dressing over the the salad and garnish with the reserved parsley. Serve at once.

cooks tip

For a really quick salad, use a frozen packet of mixed vegetables, thawed, instead of fresh vegetables.

potato, mixed bean & apple salad

Use any mixture of beans you have to hand in this recipe; the wider the variety, the more colorful the salad.

Serves 4

8 oz new potatoes, scrubbed and quartered

8 oz mixed canned beans, such as red
    kidney beans, small navy, and borlotti
    beans, drained and rinsed

1 red dessert apple, diced and tossed in
    1 tbsp lemon juice

1 small yellow bell pepper, diced

1 shallot, sliced

½ head fennel, sliced

oak leaf lettuce leaves

DRESSING

1 tbsp red wine vinegar

2 tbsp olive oil

½ tbsp American mustard

1 garlic clove, finely chopped

2 tsp chopped fresh thyme

2

3

4

1 Cook the quartered potatoes in a pan of boiling water for 15 minutes until tender. Drain and transfer to a mixing bowl.

2 Add the mixed beans to the potatoes with the diced apple and yellow bell pepper, and the sliced shallots and fennel. Mix well, taking care not to break up the cooked potatoes.

3 In a bowl, whisk all the dressing ingredients together, then pour it over the potato salad.

4 Line a plate or salad bowl with the oak leaf lettuce and spoon the potato mixture into the center. Serve immediately.

cook's tip

Canned beans are used here for convenience, but dried beans may be used instead. Soak for 8 hours or overnight, drain, and place in a saucepan. Cover with water, bring to a boil, and boil for 10 minutes, then simmer until tender.

variation

Use Dijon or whole-grain mustard in place of American mustard for a different flavor.

bean curd & vegetable stir-fry

This is a quick dish to prepare, making it ideal as a mid-week supper dish after a busy day at work!

Serves 4

1¼ cups potatoes, cubed

1 tbsp olive oil

1 red onion, sliced

8 oz firm bean curd, diced

2 zucchini, diced

8 canned artichoke hearts, halved

⅔ cup sieved tomatoes

1 tsp superfine sugar

2 tbsp chopped basil

salt and pepper

3

cook's tip

Canned artichoke hearts should be drained thoroughly and rinsed before use because they often have salt added.

1 Cook the potatoes in a pan of boiling water for 10 minutes. Drain thoroughly and set aside until required.

2 Heat the oil in a large skillet and sauté the red onion for 2 minutes until the onion has softened, stirring.

3 Stir in the bean curd and zucchini and cook for 3–4 minutes until they begin to brown slightly. Add the potatoes, stirring to mix.

3

4 Stir in the artichoke hearts, sieved tomatoes, sugar, and basil, season with salt and pepper and cook for a further 5 minutes, stirring well. Transfer the stir-fry to serving dishes and serve immediately.

variation

Eggplants could be used instead of the zucchini, if preferred.

4

indonesian potato & chicken salad

The spicy peanut dressing served with this salad may be prepared in advance and left to chill a day before required.

Serves 4

4 large waxy potatoes, diced

10 oz fresh pineapple, diced

2 carrots, grated

6 oz beansprouts

1 bunch scallions, sliced

1 large zucchini, cut into matchsticks

3 celery stalks, cut into matchsticks

6 oz unsalted peanuts

2 cooked chicken breast fillets, about 4½ oz
    each, sliced

6 tbsp crunchy peanut butter

6 tbsp olive oil

2 tbsp light soy sauce

1 red chile, chopped

2 tsp sesame oil

4 tsp lime juice

lemon wedges, to garnish

3

4

1 Cook the diced potatoes in a pan of boiling water for 10 minutes or until tender. Drain and leave to cool.

2 Transfer the cooled potatoes to a salad bowl.

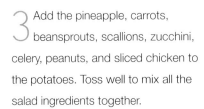

3 Add the pineapple, carrots, beansprouts, scallions, zucchini, celery, peanuts, and sliced chicken to the potatoes. Toss well to mix all the salad ingredients together.

4 To make the dressing, put the peanut butter in a small bowl and gradually whisk in the olive oil and light soy sauce.

5

5 Stir in the chopped red chile, sesame oil and lime juice. Mix until well combined.

6 Pour the spicy dressing over the salad and toss lightly to coat all of the ingredients. Serve the salad immediately, garnished with the lime wedges.

cook's tip

Unsweetened canned pineapple may be used in place of the fresh pineapple if it is more convenient. If only sweetened canned pineapple is available, drain it and rinse under cold running water before using.

old english spicy chicken salad

For this simple, refreshing summer salad you can use leftover roast chicken, or ready-roasted chicken to save time. Add the dressing just before serving, or the spinach will lost its crispness.

2

3

Serves 4

9 oz young spinach leaves

3 stalks celery, sliced thinly

½ cucumber

2 scallions

3 tbsp chopped fresh parsley

12 oz boneless, roast chicken,

   sliced thinly

DRESSING

1 inch piece gingerroot, grated finely

3 tbsp olive oil

1 tbsp white wine vinegar

1 tbsp clear honey

½ tsp ground cinnamon

salt and pepper

smoked almonds, to garnish (optional)

1 Thoroughly wash the spinach leaves, then pat dry with paper towels.

2 Using a sharp knife, thinly slice the celery, cucumber, and scallion. Toss in a large bowl with the spinach leaves and parsley.

3 Transfer to serving plates and arrange the chicken on top of the salad.

4

4 In a screw-topped jar, combine all the dressing ingredients and shake well to mix. Season the dressing with salt and pepper to taste, then pour over the salad. Sprinkle with a few smoked almonds, if using.

variation

Substitute corn salad for the spinach, if you prefer.

variation

Fresh young spinach leaves go particularly well with fruit — try adding a few fresh raspberries or nectarine slices to make an even more refreshing salad.

potato & italian sausage salad

Sliced Italian sausage blends well with the other strong, Mediterranean flavors of sun-dried tomato and basil in this salad. All of the flavors are relatively strong and therefore do not overpower each other.

Serves 4

1 lb waxy potatoes

1 raddichio or lollo rosso lettuce

1 green bell pepper, sliced

6 oz Italian sausage, sliced

1 red onion, halved and sliced

4½ oz sun-dried tomatoes, sliced

2 tbsp shredded fresh basil

1 tbsp balsamic vinegar

1 tsp tomato paste

2 tbsp olive oil

salt and pepper

1 Cook the potatoes in a pan of boiling water for 20 minutes or until cooked through. Drain and leave to cool.

2 Line a large serving platter with the radicchio or lollo rosso lettuce leaves.

3 Slice the cooled potatoes and arrange them in layers on the lettuce-lined serving platter together with the sliced green bell pepper, sliced Italian sausage, red onion, sun-dried tomatoes, and shredded fresh basil.

4 In a small bowl, whisk the balsamic vinegar, tomato paste, and olive oil together and season to taste with salt and pepper. Pour the dressing over the potato salad and serve immediately.

3

3

cook's tip

You can use either packets of sun-dried tomatoes or jars of sun-dried tomatoes in oil. If using tomatoes packed in oil, simply rinse the oil from the tomatoes and pat them dry on paper towels before using.

3

variation

Any sliced Italian sausage or salami can be used in this salad. Italy is home of the salami and there are numerous varieties to choose from — those from the south tend to be more highly spiced than those from the north of the country.

4

chinese shrimp salad

Noodles and beansprouts form the basis of this refreshing salad which combines the flavors of fruit and shrimp for a quick and delicious dish.

Serves 4

9 oz fine egg noodles

3 tbsp sunflower oil

1 tbsp sesame oil

1 tbsp sesame seeds

1¼ cups beansprouts

1 ripe mango, sliced

6 scallions, sliced

2¾ oz radishes, sliced

12 oz peeled cooked shrimp

2 tbsp light soy sauce

1 tbsp sherry

3

4

5

variation

If fresh mango is unavailable, use canned mango slices, rinsed and drained, instead.

1 Place the egg noodles in a large bowl and pour over enough boiling water to cover. Leave to stand for 10 minutes.

2 Drain the noodles thoroughly and pat away any moisture with absorbent paper towels.

3 Heat the sunflower oil in a large wok. Add the noodles and stir-fry for 5 minutes, tossing frequently.

4 Remove the wok from the heat and add the sesame oil, sesame seeds and beansprouts, tossing to mix well.

5 In a separate bowl, mix together the sliced mango, scallions, radishes, shrimp, light soy sauce, and sherry.

6 Toss the shrimp mixture with the noodles or alternatively, arrange the noodles around the edge of a serving plate and pile the shrimp mixture into the center. Serve immediately.

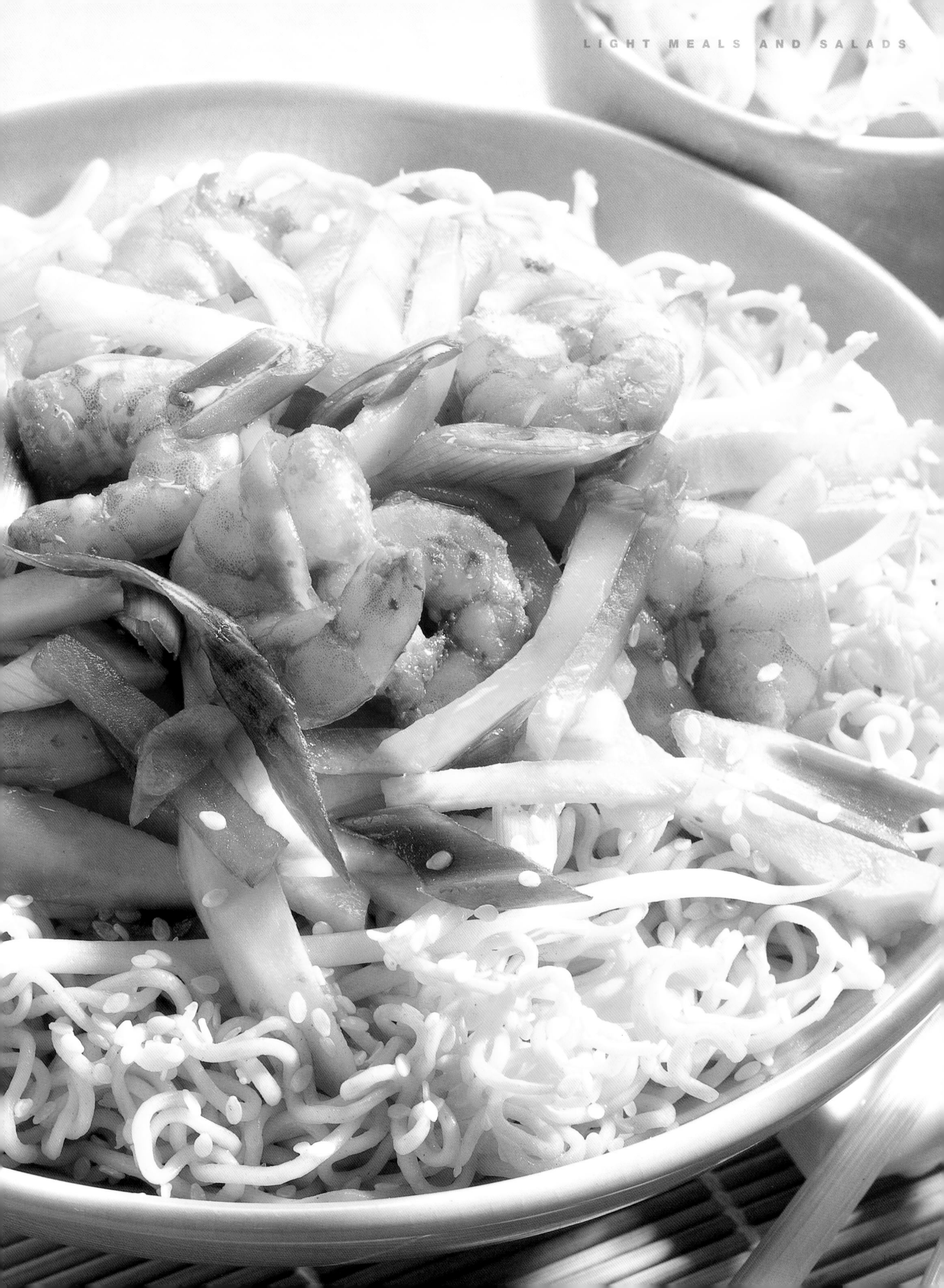

lentil & tuna salad

In this recipe, lentils, combined with spices, lemon juice, and tuna, make a wonderfully tasty and filling salad.

Serves 4

2 ripe tomatoes

1 small red onion

3 tbsp virgin olive oil

1 tbsp lemon juice

1 tsp whole-grain mustard

1 garlic clove, finely chopped

½ tsp cumin powder

½ tsp ground coriander

1 x 14 oz can lentils, drained

1 x 6¼ can tuna, drained

2 tbsp fresh cilantro, chopped

pepper

1

cook's tip

Lentils are a good source of protein and contain important vitamins and minerals. Buy them dried for soaking and cooking yourself, or buy canned varieties for speed and convenience.

3

1 Using a sharp knife, seed the tomatoes and chop them into fine dice.

2 Using a sharp knife, finely chop the red onion.

3 To make the dressing, whisk together the virgin olive oil, lemon juice, mustard, garlic, cumin powder, and ground coriander in a small bowl. Set aside until required.

4 Mix together the chopped onion, diced tomatoes, and drained lentils in a large bowl.

5 Flake the tuna and stir it into the onion, tomato, and lentil mixture.

6 Stir in the chopped fresh cilantro.

7 Pour the dressing over the lentil and tuna salad and season with freshly ground black pepper. Serve at once.

4

variation

Nuts would add extra flavor and texture to this salad.

For poultry lovers this chapter contains pasta dishes, risottos and bakes, incorporating a range of healthy and colorful ingredients. Classic and traditional many of the meat dishes on offer may be, but they are all speedy to make, and use ingredients that can be pantry staples. Others have a modern twist but are equally simple to prepare. The dishes in this chapter range from easy, economic mid-week suppers to quick but sophisticated and elegant main courses for special

occasions. All of the recipes are extremely wholesome, offering a comprehensive range of tastes. Those on a low-fat diet should use lean cuts of meat and look out for low-fat ground meat to enjoy the dishes featured here.

meat & poultry

ham steaks with spicy apple rings

This dish is quick to prepare because there is no marinating involved.
Ham has a good, strong flavor and cooks well on the grill.

1

3

5

Serves 4

4 ham steaks, each about 6 oz

1–2 tsp whole-grain mustard

1 tbsp honey

2 tbsp lemon juice

1 tbsp sunflower oil

2 green dessert apples

2 tsp demerara sugar

¼ tsp ground nutmeg

¼ tsp ground cinnamon

¼ tsp ground allspice

1–2 tbsp melted butter

1 Using a pair of scissors, make a few cuts around the edges of the ham steaks to prevent them from curling up as they cook. Spread a little whole-grain mustard over the steaks.

2 Mix together the honey, lemon juice, and oil in a bowl.

3 To prepare the apple rings, core the apples and cut them into thick slices. Mix the sugar with the spices and press the apple slices in the mixture until well coated on both sides.

4 Grill the steaks over hot coals for 3–4 minutes on each side, basting with the honey and lemon mixture.

5 Brush the apple slices with a little melted butter and grill alongside the ham for 3–4 minutes, turning once and brushing with melted butter as they cook.

6 Serve the ham steaks with the apple slices as a garnish.

cook's tip

Ham can be a little salty. If you have time, soak the steaks in cold water for 30-60 minutes before cooking — this process will remove the excess salt.

variation

Pineapple rings can also be cooked in the same way as the apple rings for a delicious alternative garnish to this dish.

pork tenderloin stir-fry with crunchy satay sauce

Satay sauce is easy to make and is one of the best known sauces in Asian cooking.

Serves 4

5½ oz carrots

2 tbsp sunflower oil

12 oz pork neck tenderloin, thinly sliced

1 onion, sliced

3 cloves garlic, finely chopped

1 yellow bell pepper, seeded and sliced

2¼ cups snow peas

1½ cups fine asparagus

6 tbsp crunchy peanut butter

6 tbsp coconut milk

1 tsp chili flakes

1 tsp tomato paste

chopped salted peanuts, to serve

1

2

3

1 Using a sharp knife, slice the carrots into thin sticks.

2 Heat the oil in a large wok. Add the pork, onion and ⅔ of the garlic and stir-fry for 5 minutes or until the pork is cooked through.

3 Add the carrots, bell pepper, snow peas, and asparagus to the wok and stir-fry for 5 minutes.

4 To make the satay sauce, place the peanut butter, coconut milk, chili flakes, remaining garlic, and tomato paste in a small pan and heat gently, stirring, until well combined.

5 Transfer the stir-fry to warm serving plates. Spoon the satay sauce over the stir-fry and scatter with chopped peanuts. Serve immediately.

cook's tip

Cook the sauce just before serving as it tends to thicken very quickly and will not be spoonable if you cook it too far in advance.

honey-glazed pork chops

The addition of freshly grated ginger gives a delicious tang to the honey-flavored glaze. Make sure the pork is cooked through before serving.

Serves 6

4 lean pork loin chops

salt and pepper

4 tbsp clear honey

1 tbsp dry sherry

4 tbsp orange juice

2 tbsp olive oil

1 inch piece gingerroot, grated

1 Season the pork chops with salt and pepper to taste. Set aside while you make the glaze.

2 To make the glaze, place the honey, sherry, orange juice, oil, and ginger in a small pan and heat gently, stirring continuously, until all of the ingredients are well blended.

3 Grill the chops on an oiled rack over hot coals for about 5 minutes on each side.

4 Brush the chops with the glaze and grill for a further 2–4 minutes on each side, basting frequently with the glaze.

5 Transfer the chops to warm serving plates and serve hot.

variation

This recipe works equally well with lamb chops and with chicken portions, such as thighs or drumsticks. Grill the meat in exactly the same way as in this recipe, basting frequently with the honey glaze – the result will be just as delicious!

cook's tip

To give the recipe a little more punch, stir ½ tsp of chili sauce or 1 tbsp of whole-grain mustard to the basting glaze.

2

3

4

neapolitan pork steaks

An Italian version of grilled pork steaks, this dish is easy to make and delicious to eat. Serve with fresh, green vegetables.

There are many types of canned tomato available — for example plum tomatoes, or tomatoes chopped in water, or chopped sieved passata. The chopped variety are often canned with added flavors such as garlic, basil, onion, chili, and mixed herbs, and are a good pantry standby.

Serves 4

2 tbsp olive oil

1 large onion, sliced

1 garlic clove, chopped

1 x 14 oz can tomatoes

2 tsp yeast extract

4 pork loin steaks, each about 4½ oz

2¾ oz black olives, pitted

2 tbsp fresh basil, shredded

freshly grated Parmesan cheese, to serve

1 Heat the oil in a large skillet. Add the onion and garlic and sauté, stirring, for 3–4 minutes or until they just begin to soften.

2 Add the tomatoes and yeast extract to the skillet and leave to simmer for about 5 minutes or until the sauce starts to thicken.

1

2

3 Cook the pork steaks, under a preheated broiler, for 5 minutes on both sides, until the the meat is golden and cooked through. Set the pork steaks aside and keep warm.

4 Add the olives and fresh shredded basil to the sauce in the skillet and stir quickly to combine.

4

5 Transfer the steaks to warm serving plates. Top the steaks with the sauce, sprinkle with freshly grated Parmesan cheese and serve immediately.

cook's tip

Parmesan is a mature and exceptionally hard cheese produced in Italy. You only need to add a little as it has a very strong flavor.

orecchioni with pork in cream sauce

This unusual and attractive dish is surprisingly quick and easy to make.
Don't be deterred by the quail eggs; they are simple to cook.

Serves 4

1 lb pork tenderloin, thinly sliced

4 tbsp olive oil

8 oz white mushrooms, sliced

⅔ cup Italian red wine sauce

1 tbsp lemon juice

pinch of saffron

3 cups dried orecchioni

4 tbsp heavy cream

12 quail eggs (see Cook's Tip, below)

salt

1

3

6

1 Pound the slices of pork between 2 sheets of plastic wrap until they are wafer thin, then cut into strips.

2 Heat the olive oil in a large skillet, add the pork and stir-fry for 5 minutes. Add the mushrooms to the pan and stir-fry for a further 2 minutes.

3 Pour over the Italian red wine sauce, lower the heat, and simmer gently for 20 minutes.

4 Meanwhile, bring a large pan of lightly salted water to a boil. Add the lemon juice, saffron, and orecchioni and cook for 12 minutes, until tender but still firm to the bite. Drain the pasta and keep warm.

5 Stir the cream into the pan with the pork and heat gently for a few minutes.

6 Boil the quail eggs for 3 minutes, cool them in cold water and remove the shells.

7 Transfer the pasta to a large, warm serving plate, top with the pork and the sauce and garnish with the eggs. Serve immediately.

cook's tip

In this recipe, the quail eggs are soft-cooked. As they are extremely difficult to shell when warm, it is important that they are thoroughly cooled first. Otherwise, they will break up unattractively.

caribbean pork

This unusual dish combines the sweetness of fruit juices with the sharpness of rum. It is excellent served with typically Caribbean coconut rice.

2

4

5

Serves 6

4 pork loin chops

4 tbsp dark muscovado sugar

4 tbsp orange or pineapple juice

2 tbsp Jamaican rum

1 tbsp crushed coconut

1 tsp ground cinnamon

1 cup Basmati rice

2 cups water

1 cup coconut milk

4 tbsp raisins

4 tbsp roasted peanuts

salt and pepper

2 tbsp crushed coconut, toasted

mixed salad leaves, to serve

1 Trim any excess fat from the pork and place the chops in a shallow, non-metallic dish.

2 Combine the sugar, fruit juice, rum, coconut, and cinnamon in a bowl, stirring until the sugar dissolves. Pour the mixture over the pork and leave to marinate in the refrigerator for at least two hours.

3 Remove the pork from the marinade, reserving the liquid for basting. Grill over hot coals for 15-20 minutes, basting with the marinade.

4 Meanwhile, make the coconut rice. Rinse the rice under cold water, place it in a pan with the water and coconut milk, and bring it gently to a boil. Stir, cover, and reduce the heat. Simmer gently for 12 minutes or until the rice is tender and the liquid has been absorbed. Fluff up with a fork.

5 Stir the raisins and nuts into the rice, season with salt and pepper to taste, and sprinkle with the coconut. Transfer the pork and rice to warm serving plates and serve with the mixed salad leaves.

pork fry with vegetables

This is a very simple dish which lends itself to almost any combination of vegetables that you have to hand.

Serves 4

12 oz lean pork tenderloin

2 tbsp vegetable oil

2 garlic cloves, finely chopped

½-inch piece gingerroot, cut into slivers

1 carrot, cut into thin strips

1 red bell pepper, seeded and diced

1 fennel bulb, sliced

1 oz water chestnuts, halved

2¼ oz beansprouts

2 tbsp Chinese rice wine

1¼ cups pork or chicken stock

pinch of dark brown sugar

1 tsp cornstarch

2 tsp water

cook's tip

Use dry sherry instead of the Chinese rice wine if you have difficulty obtaining it.

1 Cut the pork into thin slices. Heat the oil in a preheated wok. Add the garlic, gingerroot, and pork and stir-fry for 1–2 minutes, until the meat is sealed.

2 Add the carrot, bell pepper, fennel, and water chestnuts to the wok and stir-fry for about 2-3 minutes.

3 Add the beansprouts and stir-fry for 1 minute. Remove the pork and vegetables from the wok and keep warm.

4 Add the Chinese rice wine, pork or chicken stock, and sugar to the wok. Blend the cornstarch to a smooth paste with the water and stir it into the sauce. Bring to a boil, stirring constantly until thickened and clear.

5 Return the meat and vegetables to the wok and cook for 1–2 minutes, until heated through and coated with the sauce. Transfer to a warm serving dish and serve immediately.

2

2

4

twice-cooked pork with bell peppers

This is a really simple yet colorful dish, the trio of bell peppers off-setting the pork and sauce wonderfully.

Serves 4

½ oz dried shiitake mushrooms

1 lb pork leg steaks

2 tbsp vegetable oil

1 onion, sliced

1 red bell pepper, seeded and diced

1 green bell pepper, seeded and diced

1 yellow bell pepper, seeded and diced

4 tbsp oyster sauce

variation

Use open-cap mushrooms, sliced, instead of shiitake mushrooms, if you prefer.

1 Place the mushrooms in a large bowl. Pour over enough boiling water to cover and leave to stand for 20 minutes.

2 Using a sharp knife, trim any excess fat from the pork steaks. Cut the pork into thin strips.

3 Bring a large saucepan of water to a boil. Add the pork to a boiling water and cook for 5 minutes.

4 Remove the pork from the pan with a draining spoon and leave to drain thoroughly.

5 Heat the oil in a large preheated wok. Add the pork to the wok and stir-fry for about 5 minutes.

6 Remove the mushrooms from the water and leave to drain thoroughly. Roughly chop the mushrooms.

7 Add the mushrooms, onion and the bell peppers to the wok and stir-fry for 5 minutes.

8 Stir in the oyster sauce and cook for 2-3 minutes. Transfer to serving bowls and serve immediately.

2

3

7

sweet lamb tenderloin

Lamb tenderloin, enhanced by a sweet and spicy glaze, is cooked
in a kitchen foil packet for deliciously moist results.

3

Serves 4

2 lamb tenderloins, each 8 oz

salt and pepper

1 tbsp olive oil

½ onion, chopped finely

1 clove garlic, finely chopped

1 inch piece gingerroot, grated

5 tbsp apple juice

3 tbsp smooth apple sauce

1 tbsp light muscovado sugar

1 tbsp tomato catsup

½ tsp mild mustard

green salad greens, croutons, and fresh
    crusty bread, to serve

cook's tip

If you prefer, you can cook
the lamb for the first part
of the cooking time in a
preheated oven at 350°F.
Place the kitchen foil packet
in a baking dish to avoid
any leakages.

4

1 Place the lamb tenderloin on a large piece of double thickness kitchen foil. Season with salt and pepper to taste.

2 Heat the oil in a small skillet and sauté the onion and garlic for 2–3 minutes until soft but not browned. Stir in the grated gingerroot and cook for 1 minute, stirring occasionally.

3 Stir in the apple juice, apple sauce, sugar, catsup, and mustard and bring to a boil. Boil rapidly for about 10 minutes until reduced by half. Stir the mixture occasionally so that it does not burn and stick to the bottom.

4 Brush half of the sauce over the lamb, then wrap up the lamb in the kitchen foil to enclose it completely. Grill over hot coals for about 25 minutes, turning the packet over from time to time.

5

5 Open out the kitchen foil and brush the lamb with some of the sauce. Continue to grill for a further 15–20 minutes or until cooked through.

6 Place the lamb on a chopping board, remove the foil, and cut into thick slices. Transfer to serving plates and spoon over the remaining sauce. Serve with green salad greens, croutons, and fresh crusty bread.

scallion & lamb stir-fry with oyster sauce

This really is a speedy dish, lamb leg steaks being perfect for the short cooking time. The sauces are quite salty, so no extra salt is needed.

Serves 4

1 lb lamb leg steaks

1 tsp ground Szechuan peppercorns

1 tbsp peanut oil

2 cloves garlic, finely chopped

8 scallions, sliced

2 tbsp dark soy sauce

6 tbsp oyster sauce

6 oz Chinese cabbage

shrimp crackers, to serve

cook's tip

Shrimp crackers consist of compressed slivers of shrimp and flour paste. They expand when deep-fried.

2

3

1 Using a sharp knife, remove any excess fat from the lamb. Slice the lamb thinly.

2 Sprinkle the ground Szechuan peppercorns over the meat and toss together until well combined.

3 Heat the oil in a preheated wok. Add the lamb and stir-fry for 5 minutes.

4

4 Mix the garlic, scallions, and soy, add to the wok and stir-fry for 2 minutes.

5 Add the oyster sauce and Chinese leaves and stir-fry for a further 2 minutes, or until the leaves have wilted and the juices are bubbling.

6 Transfer the stir-fry to serving bowls and serve hot with shrimp crackers.

cook's tip

Oyster sauce is made from oysters which are cooked in brine and soy sauce. Sold in bottles, it will keep in the refrigerator for months.

sesame lamb stir-fry

This is a very simple, but delicious dish, in which lean pieces of lamb are cooked in sugar and soy sauce and sprinkled with sesame seeds, then served on a bed of leeks and carrot.

1

2

3

Serves 4

1 lb boneless lean lamb

2 tbsp peanut oil

2 leeks, sliced

1 carrot, cut into matchsticks

2 garlic cloves, finely chopped

½ cup lamb or vegetable stock

2 tsp light brown sugar

1 tbsp dark soy sauce

4½ tsp sesame seeds

1 Cut the lamb into thin strips. Heat the peanut oil in a preheated wok. Add the lamb and stir-fry for 2–3 minutes. Remove the lamb from the wok with a draining spoon and set aside.

2 Add the leek, carrot, and garlic to the wok and stir-fry in the remaining oil for 1–2 minutes. Remove from the wok with a draining spoon and set aside. Drain any remaining oil from the wok.

3 Place the lamb or vegetable stock, sugar, and soy sauce in the wok and add the lamb. Cook, stirring constantly to coat the lamb, for 2–3 minutes. Sprinkle the sesame seeds over the top, turning the lamb to coat.

4 Spoon the leek mixture on to a warm serving dish and top with the lamb. Serve immediately.

cook's tip

Be careful not to burn the sugar in the wok when heating and coating the meat, otherwise the flavor of the dish will be spoiled.

variation

This recipe would be equally delicious made with strips of skinless chicken or turkey breast or with shrimp. The cooking times remain the same.

lamb cutlets with rosemary

A classic combination of flavors, this dish would make a perfect Sunday lunch. Serve with tomato and onion salad and jacket potatoes.

1

4

5

Serves 4

8 lamb cutlets

5 tbsp olive oil

2 tbsp lemon juice

1 clove garlic, finely chopped

½ tsp lemon pepper

salt

8 sprigs rosemary

jacket potatoes, to serve

4 tomatoes, sliced

4 scallions, sliced diagonally

DRESSING

2 tbsp olive oil

1 tbsp lemon juice

1 clove garlic, chopped

¼ tsp fresh rosemary, chopped finely

1 Trim the lamb chops by cutting away the flesh with a sharp knife to expose the tips of the bones.

2 Place the oil, lemon juice, garlic, lemon pepper, and salt in a shallow, non-metallic dish and whisk with a fork to combine.

3 Lay the sprigs of rosemary in the dish and place the lamb on top. Leave to marinate for at least 1 hour, turning the lamb cutlets once.

4 Remove the chops from the marinade and wrap a little kitchen foil around the bones to stop them from burning.

5 Place the sprigs of rosemary on the rack and place the lamb on top. Grill for 10–15 minutes, turning once.

6 Meanwhile make the salad and dressing. Arrange the tomatoes on a serving dish and scatter the scallions on top. Place all the ingredients for the dressing in a screw-top jar, shake well and pour over the salad. Serve with the grilled lamb cutlets and jacket potatoes.

cook's tip

Choose medium to small baking potatoes if you want to cook jacket potatoes on the grill. Scrub them well, prick with a fork and wrap in buttered kitchen foil. Bury them in the hot coals and grill for 50-60 minutes.

lean lamb cooked in spinach

Serve this nutritious combination of lamb and spinach with plain boiled rice to bring out the flavor.

Serves 2-4

1¼ cups oil

2 medium onions, sliced

¼ bunch fresh cilantro

3 green chiles, chopped

1½ tsp fresh gingerroot, finely chopped

1½ tsp fresh garlic, finely chopped

1 tsp chili powder

½ tsp turmeric

1 lb lean lamb, cubed

1 tsp salt

2 lb fresh spinach, trimmed, washed, and
    chopped or 15 oz can spinach

3½ cups water

fresh gingerroot, peeled and shredded, and
    fresh cilantro leaves, to garnish

1 Heat the oil in a deep skillet and sauté the onions until they turn a pale color.

2 Add the fresh cilantro and 2 of the chopped green chiles to the pan and stir-fry for 3-5 minutes.

3 Reduce the heat and add the gingerroot, garlic, chili powder, and turmeric to the mixture in the pan, stirring to mix.

4 Add the lamb to the pan and stir-fry for a further 5 minutes. Add the salt and the fresh or canned spinach and cook, stirring occasionally with a wooden spoon, for a further 3-5 minutes.

5 Add the water, stirring, and cook over a low heat, covered, for about 45 minutes. Remove the lid and check the meat. If it is not tender, turn the meat over, increase the heat and cook, uncovered, until the surplus water has been absorbed. Stir-fry the mixture for a further 5-7 minutes.

6 Transfer the lamb and spinach mixture to a serving dish and garnish with shredded gingerroot, fresh cilantro leaves and the remaining chopped green chile. Serve hot.

2

3

4

stir-fried lamb with orange

Oranges and lamb are a great combination because the citrus flavor off-sets the fattier, fuller flavor of the lamb.

Serves 4

1 lb ground lamb

2 cloves garlic, finely chopped

1 tsp cumin seeds

1 tsp ground coriander

1 red onion, sliced

finely grated zest and juice of 1 orange

2 tbsp soy sauce

1 orange, peeled and segmented

salt and pepper

snipped fresh chives, to garnish

cook's tip

If you wish to serve wine with your meal, try light, dry white wines and lighter Burgundy-style red wines as they blend well with oriental food.

1

2

3

1 Add the ground lamb to a preheated wok. Dry fry the ground lamb for 5 minutes, or until the meat is evenly browned. Drain away any excess fat from the wok.

2 Add the garlic, cumin seeds, coriander, and red onion to the wok and stir-fry for a further 5 minutes.

3 Stir in the finely grated orange zest and juice and the soy sauce, cover, reduce the heat, and leave to simmer, stirring occasionally, for 15 minutes.

4 Remove the lid, raise the heat, add the orange segments, and salt and pepper to taste and heat through for a further 2–3 minutes.

5 Transfer to warm serving plates and garnish with snipped fresh chives. Serve immediately.

cook's tip

Use lime or lemon juice and zest instead of the orange, if you prefer.

broiled ground lamb

This is rather an unusual way of cooking ground meat. In India this is cooked on a naked flame, but it works just as well cooked under a broiler.

Serves 4

5 tbsp oil

2 onions, sliced

1 lb ground lamb

2 tbsp yogurt

1 tsp chili powder

1 tsp fresh gingerroot, finely chopped

1 tsp fresh garlic, finely chopped

1 tsp salt

1½ tsp garam masala

½ tsp ground allspice

2 fresh green chiles

fresh cilantro leaves

1 onion, cut into rings, fresh cilantro leaves,
    chopped, and 1 lemon, cut into wedges,
    to garnish

2

3

4

1 Heat the oil in a saucepan.
Add the onions and sauté until
golden brown.

2 Place the ground lamb in a large
bowl. Add the yogurt, chili powder,
gingerroot, garlic, salt, garam masala,
ground allspice, and mix to combine.

3 Add the lamb mixture to the sautéed
onions and stir-fry for 10-15 minutes.
Remove from the heat and set aside.

4 Meanwhile, place the green chilies
and half of the cilantro leaves in a
processor and grind. Alternatively, finely
chop the green chiles and cilantro with a
sharp knife. Set aside until required.

5 Put the ground lamb mixture in
a food processor and grind.
Alternatively, place in a large bowl
and mash with a fork. Mix the lamb
mixture with the chiles and cilantro
and blend well.

6 Transfer the mixture to a shallow
heatproof dish. Cook under a
preheated medium-hot broiler for
10-15 minutes, moving the mixture
about with a fork. Watch it carefully to
prevent it from burning.

7 Serve garnished with onion rings,
cilantro, and lemon wedges.

lamb with mushroom sauce

Use a lean cut of lamb, such as tenderloin, for this recipe for both flavor and tenderness. It needs only very plain accompaniments, such as boiled rice.

Serves 4

12 oz lean boneless lamb, such
    as tenderloin

2 tbsp vegetable oil

3 garlic cloves, finely chopped

1 leek, sliced

1 tsp cornstarch

4 tbsp light soy sauce

3 tbsp Chinese rice wine or dry sherry

3 tbsp water

½ tsp chili sauce

6 oz large mushrooms, sliced

½ tsp sesame oil

fresh red chiles, to garnish

1

1 Using a sharp knife, cut the lamb into thin strips.

2 Heat the oil in a preheated wok. Add the lamb strips, garlic, and leek and stir-fry for about 2-3 minutes.

3 Mix together the cornstarch, soy sauce, Chinese rice wine or dry sherry, water, and chili sauce in a bowl and set aside.

4 Add the mushrooms to the wok and stir-fry for 1 minute.

5 Stir in the sauce and cook for 2–3 minutes, or until the lamb is cooked through and tender. Sprinkle the sesame oil over the top and transfer to a warm serving dish. Garnish with red chiles and serve immediately.

4

5

variation

The lamb can be replaced with lean steak or pork tenderloin in this classic recipe from Beijing. You could also use 2-3 scallions, 1 shallot, or 1 small onion instead of the leek, if you prefer.

cook's tip

Use rehydrated dried Chinese mushrooms obtainable from specialist stores or Chinese supermarkets for a really authentic flavor.

creamed strips of sirloin with rigatoni

This quick and easy dish tastes superb and would make a delicious treat for a special occasion. Don't stint on the quality of the steak.

1

Serves 4

6 tbsp butter

1 lb sirloin steak, trimmed and cut into
   thin strips

6 oz white mushrooms, sliced

1 tsp mustard

pinch of freshly grated gingerroot

salt and pepper

2 tbsp dry sherry

¾ cup heavy cream

1 lb dried rigatoni

2 tbsp olive oil

2 fresh basil sprigs

8 tbsp butter

4 slices hot toast, cut into triangles, to serve

2

2

cook's tip

Dried pasta will keep for up
to 6 months. Keep it in the
packet and reseal it once you
have opened it, or transfer
the pasta to an airtight jar.

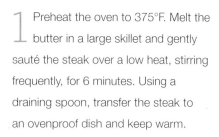

1 Preheat the oven to 375°F. Melt the butter in a large skillet and gently sauté the steak over a low heat, stirring frequently, for 6 minutes. Using a draining spoon, transfer the steak to an ovenproof dish and keep warm.

2 Add the sliced mushrooms to the skillet and cook for 2–3 minutes in the juices remaining in the pan. Add the mustard, grated gingerroot, salt, and pepper. Cook for 2 minutes, then add the sherry and cream. Cook for a further 3 minutes, then pour the cream sauce over the steak.

3 Bake the steak and cream mixture in the preheated oven for 10 minutes.

4 Meanwhile, cook the pasta. Bring a large saucepan of lightly salted water to a boil. Add the rigatoni, olive oil, and 1 of the basil sprigs and boil rapidly for 10 minutes, until tender but still firm to the bite. Drain the pasta and transfer to a warm serving plate. Toss the pasta with the butter and garnish with a sprig of basil.

5 Serve the steak with the pasta and triangles of warm toast.

beef & beans

This is a dish with an authentic Asian flavor. The green of the beans complements the dark color of the beef, served in a rich sauce.

Serves 4

2 tsp cornstarch

2 tbsp dark soy sauce

2 tsp peanut oil

1 lb rump or steak tenderloin, cut
    into 1 inch pieces

2 tbsp vegetable oil

3 garlic cloves, finely chopped

1 small onion, cut into 8

8 oz thin dwarf beans, halved

¼ cup unsalted cashew nuts

1 oz canned bamboo shoots, drained
    and rinsed

2 tsp dark soy sauce

2 tsp Chinese rice wine or dry sherry

½ cup beef stock

2 tsp cornstarch

4 tsp water

salt and pepper

1 To make the marinade, mix together
the cornstarch, soy sauce, and
peanut oil.

2 Place the steak in a shallow glass
bowl. Pour the marinade over the
steak, turn to coat thoroughly, cover,
and leave to marinate in the refrigerator
for at least 30 minutes.

2

3

3 To make the sauce, heat the oil in
a preheated wok. Add the garlic,
onion, beans, cashew nuts, and
bamboo shoots and stir-fry for 2–3
minutes.

4 Remove the steak from the
marinade, drain, add to the wok,
and stir-fry for 3–4 minutes.

5 Mix the soy sauce, Chinese rice
wine or sherry, and beef stock
together. Blend the cornstarch with the
water and add to the soy sauce mixture,
mixing to combine.

6 Stir the mixture into the wok and
bring the sauce to a boil, stirring
until thickened and clear. Reduce the
heat and leave to simmer for 2–3
minutes. Season to taste and serve
immediately.

6

variation

This recipe would also be
delicious with the addition
of sugar snap peas instead of
the beans, if you prefer.

egg noodles with beef

Quick and easy, this mouth-watering Chinese-style noodle dish can be cooked in minutes.

Serves 4

10 oz egg noodles

3 tbsp walnut oil

1 inch piece gingerroot, cut into thin strips

5 scallions, finely shredded

2 garlic cloves, finely chopped

1 red bell pepper, cored, seeded, and
   thinly sliced

3½ oz white mushrooms, thinly sliced

12 oz steak tenderloin, cut into thin strips

salt and pepper

1 tbsp cornstarch

5 tbsp dry sherry

3 tbsp soy sauce

1 tsp soft brown sugar

1 cup mung beansprouts

1 tbsp sesame oil

scallion strips, to garnish

cook's tip

If you do not have a wok, you could prepare this dish in a skillet. However, a wok is preferable, as the round base ensures an even distribution of heat and it is easier to keep stirring and tossing the contents when stir-frying.

2

1 Bring a large pan of water to a boil. Add the noodles and cook according to the directions on the packet. Drain the noodles and set aside.

2 Heat the walnut oil in a preheated wok. Add the gingerroot, scallions, and garlic and stir-fry for 45 seconds. Add the bell pepper, mushrooms, and steak and stir-fry for 4 minutes. Season to taste with salt and pepper.

3 Mix together the cornstarch, sherry, and soy sauce in a small pitcher to form a paste, and pour into the wok. Sprinkle over the brown sugar and stir-fry all of the ingredients for a further 2 minutes.

4 Add the beansprouts, drained noodles, and sesame oil to the wok, stir and toss together for 1 minute. Garnish with strips of scallion and serve immediately.

2

3

beef with green peas & black bean sauce

This recipe is the perfect example of quick stir-frying ingredients for a delicious, crisp, colorful dish.

1

Serves 4

1 lb rump steak

2 tbsp sunflower oil

1 onion

2 cloves garlic, finely chopped

1 cup fresh or frozen English peas

5¼ oz jar black bean sauce

5¼ oz Chinese cabbage, shredded

1 Using a sharp knife, trim away any fat from the beef. Cut the beef into thin slices.

2 Heat the sunflower oil in a large preheated wok.

3 Add the beef to the wok and stir-fry for 2 minutes.

4 Using a sharp knife, peel and slice the onion.

5 Add the onion, garlic, and peas to the wok and stir-fry for a further 5 minutes.

6 Add the black bean sauce and Chinese cabbage to the mixture in the wok and heat through for a further 2 minutes.

7 Transfer to warm serving bowls and serve immediately.

3

4

cook's tip

Chinese cabbages are now widely available. They look like a pale, elongated head of lettuce with light green, tightly packed crinkly leaves.

cook's tip

Buy a chunky black bean sauce, if you can, for the best texture and flavor.

beef & broccoli stir-fry

This is a great combination of ingredients in terms of color and flavor, and it is so simple and quick to prepare.

Serves 4

8 oz lean steak, trimmed

2 garlic cloves, finely chopped

dash of chili oil

½ inch piece fresh gingerroot, grated

¼ tsp Chinese five-spice powder

2 tbsp dark soy sauce

2 tbsp vegetable oil

5 oz broccoli flowerets

1 tbsp light soy sauce

¼ cup beef stock

2 tsp cornstarch

4 tsp water

carrot strips, to garnish

cook's tip

Leave the steak to marinate for several hours for a fuller flavor. Cover and leave to marinate in the refrigerator if preparing in advance.

1

3

4

1 Cut the steak into thin strips and place in a shallow glass dish. Mix together the garlic, chili oil, grated gingerroot, Chinese five-spice powder, and soy sauce in a bowl and pour over the beef, tossing to coat the strips evenly. Leave to marinate in the refrigerator.

2 Heat 1 tablespoon of the vegetable oil in a preheated wok. Add the broccoli and stir-fry over a medium heat for 4–5 minutes. Remove from the wok and set aside.

3 Heat the remaining oil in the wok. Add the steak together with the marinade, and stir-fry for 2-3 minutes, until the steak is browned and sealed.

4 Return the broccoli to the wok and stir in the soy sauce and stock.

5 Blend the cornstarch with the water to form a smooth paste and stir it into the wok. Bring to a boil, stirring, until thickened, and clear. Cook for 1 minute.

6 Transfer the beef and broccoli stir-fry to a warm serving dish, arrange the carrot strips in a lattice on top and serve immediately.

stir-fried beef & vegetables

Beef tenderloin is perfect for stir-frying as it is so tender and lends itself to quick cooking. Take care not to overcook the vegetables.

Serves 4

2 tbsp sunflower oil

12 oz beef tenderloin, sliced

1 red onion, sliced

6 oz zucchini, sliced diagonally

6 oz carrots, thinly sliced

1 red bell pepper, seeded and sliced

1 small head Chinese cabbage, shredded

1½ cups beansprouts

8 oz can bamboo shoots, drained

½ cup cashew nuts, toasted

SAUCE

3 tbsp medium sherry

3 tbsp light soy sauce

1 tsp ground ginger

1 clove garlic, finely chopped

1 tsp cornstarch

1 tbsp tomato paste

2

3

4

1 Heat the sunflower oil in a large preheated wok.

2 Add the beef and onion to the wok and stir-fry for 4–5 minutes or until the onion begins to soften and the meat is just browning.

3 Using a sharp knife, trim the zucchini and slice diagonally.

4 Add the carrots, bell pepper, and zucchini and stir-fry for 5 minutes.

5 Toss in the Chinese cabbage, beansprouts and bamboo shoots and heat through for 2–3 minutes, or until the leaves are just beginning to wilt.

6 Scatter the cashews nuts over the stir-fry.

7 To make the sauce, mix together the sherry, soy sauce, ground ginger, garlic, cornstarch, and tomato paste. Pour the sauce over the stir-fry and toss until well combined. Allow the sauce to bubble for 2–3 minutes or until the juices start to thicken.

8 Transfer to warm serving dishes and serve at once.

spicy beef

In this recipe beef is marinated in a garlic, star anise, and soy sauce marinade for a distinctive flavor. The sauce forms a flavorsome glaze over the meat.

Serves 4

8 oz steak tenderloin

2 garlic cloves, finely chopped

1 tsp powdered star anise

1 tbsp dark soy sauce

2 tbsp vegetable oil

1 bunch scallions, halved lengthways

1 tbsp dark soy sauce

1 tbsp dry sherry

¼ tsp chili sauce

½ cup water

2 tsp cornstarch

scallion tassels, to garnish

cook's tip

Omit the chili sauce for a milder dish.

1

3

4

1 Cut the steak into thin strips and place in a shallow dish.

2 Mix together the garlic, star anise, and dark soy sauce in a bowl and pour over the steak strips, turning them to coat thoroughly. Cover and leave to marinate in the refrigerator for at least 1 hour.

3 Heat the oil in a preheated wok. Reduce the heat, add the halved scallions and stir-fry for 1-2 minutes. Remove from the wok and set aside.

4 Add the beef to the wok, together with the marinade, and stir-fry for 3–4 minutes. Return the halved scallions to the wok and add the soy sauce, sherry, chili sauce, and two-thirds of the water.

5 Blend the cornstarch to a paste with the remaining water and stir into the wok. Bring to a boil, stirring until the sauce thickens and clears.

6 Transfer to a warm serving dish, garnish with scallion tassels and serve immediately.

sautéed kidneys

Sautéed lamb kidneys are a popular dish for a late breakfast or brunch, served with paratas and a fried egg.

1

2

Serves 4

1 lb lamb's kidneys

2 tsp turmeric

2 tsp salt

1 green bell pepper, sliced

⅔ cup water

1 tsp fresh gingerroot, finely chopped

1 tsp fresh garlic, finely chopped

1 tsp chili powder

½ tsp salt

3 tbsp oil

1 small onion, finely chopped

cilantro leaves, to garnish

1 Using a sharp knife, remove the very fine skin surrounding each kidney. Cut each kidney into 4-6 pieces.

2 Place the kidney pieces in a bowl of warm water with turmeric and 2 teaspoons of salt for about 1 hour. Drain the kidneys thoroughly, then rinse them under cold running water until the water runs clear.

3 Place the kidneys in a small pan together with the green bell pepper. Pour in enough water to cover and cook over a medium heat, leaving the lid of the pan slightly ajar so that the steam can escape, until all of the water has evaporated.

4 Add the chopped gingerroot, chopped garlic, chili powder, and the rest of the salt to the kidney mixture and blend until well combined.

3

5 Add the oil, onion, and the cilantro to the pan, and stir-fry for 7-10 minutes.

6 Transfer the kidneys to a serving plate and serve hot.

liver & onion kabobs

Liver is full of iron, making this dish nutritious as well as flavorsome.
Pregnant women should take medical advice before eating liver, however.

Makes 4

12 oz lamb's liver

2 tbsp seasoned all-purpose flour

½ tsp dried mixed herbs

4½ oz rindless bacon strips

2 medium onions

2¼ oz butter

2 tsp balsamic vinegar

mixed salad leaves and tomato quarters,
    to serve

1

1 Cut the liver into bite-sized pieces.
Mix the flour with the dried herbs
and toss the liver in the seasoned flour.

2 Stretch out the bacon strips with the
back of a knife. Cut each strip in half
and wrap the bacon around half of the
liver pieces.

5

3 Thread the plain liver pieces on
to skewers, alternating with the
bacon-wrapped liver pieces.

4 Cut the onions into rings and thread
over the kabobs. Finely chop the
onion rings that are too small to thread
over the kabobs.

5 Heat the butter in a small pan and
sauté the chopped onions for about
5 minutes until soft. Stir in the vinegar.

4

6 Brush the butter mixture over the
kabobs and grill over hot coals for
8–10 minutes, basting occasionally with
the butter mixture, until the liver is just
cooked but is still a little pink inside.

7 Transfer the kabobs to serving
plates. Serve with mixed salad
leaves and tomatoes.

cook's tip

Choose thick slices of liver
to give good-sized pieces.
Use bacon to hold 2-3 pieces
of thinner liver together
if necessary.

quick chicken bake

This recipe is a type of pie and is very versatile. Add vegetables and herbs of your choice, depending on what you have at hand.

Serves 4

1 lb 2 oz ground chicken

1 large onion, chopped finely

2 carrots, diced finely

2 tbsp all-purpose flour

1 tbsp tomato paste

1¼ cups chicken stock

salt and pepper

pinch of fresh thyme

2 lb potatoes, creamed with butter and milk
   and highly seasoned

¼ cup grated hard cheese

English peas, to serve

variation

Instead of hard cheese, you could sprinkle any cheese of your choice over the top of the pie. Choose a cheese which melts easily to use as a topping. Alternatively, you could use a mixture of cheeses, depending on whatever you have at hand.

3

4

5

3 Gradually blend in the tomato paste and stock then simmer for 15 minutes. Season and add the thyme.

4 Transfer the chicken and vegetable mixture to a baking casserole and allow to cool.

5 Spoon the mashed potato over the chicken mixture and sprinkle with the hard cheese. Bake in a preheated oven at 400°F for 20 minutes, or until the cheese is bubbling and golden, then serve with the peas.

1 Dry-fry the ground chicken, onion, and carrots in a non-stick pan for 5 minutes, stirring frequently.

2 Sprinkle the chicken with the flour and simmer for a further 2 minutes.

chicken chop suey

Both well known and popular, chop suey dishes are easy to make and delicious. They are based on beansprouts and soy sauce with a meat or vegetable flavoring.

2

Serves 4

4 tbsp light soy sauce

2 tsp light brown sugar

1¼ lb skinless, boneless chicken breasts

3 tbsp vegetable oil

2 onions, quartered

2 garlic cloves, finely chopped

12 oz beansprouts

3 tsp sesame oil

1 tbsp cornstarch

3 tbsp water

2 cups chicken stock

shredded leek, to garnish

3

1 Mix the soy sauce and sugar together, stirring until the sugar has dissolved.

2 Trim any fat from the chicken and cut the meat into thin strips. Place the chicken strips in a shallow glass dish and spoon the soy mixture over them, turning to coat. Leave to marinate in the refrigerator for 20 minutes.

variation

This recipe may be made with strips of lean steak, pork, or with mixed vegetables. Change the type of stock accordingly.

3 Heat the oil in a preheated wok. Add the chicken and stir-fry for 2–3 minutes, until golden brown.

4 Add the onions and garlic and cook for a further 2 minutes. Add the beansprouts, cook for a further 4–5 minutes, then add the sesame oil.

5 Blend the cornstarch with the water to form a smooth paste. Pour the stock into the wok, together with the cornstarch paste and bring to a boil, stirring constantly until the sauce is thickened and clear. Transfer to a warm serving dish, garnish with shredded leek, and serve.

4

chicken strips & dips

Very simple to make and easy to eat with fingers, this dish can be served warm for a light lunch or cold as part of a buffet.

Serves 2

2 boneless chicken breasts

2 tbsp all-purpose flour

1 tbsp sunflower oil

PEANUT DIP

3 tbsp smooth or crunchy peanut butter

4 tbsp unsweetened yogurt

1 tsp grated orange rind

orange juice (optional)

TOMATO DIP

5 tbsp mascarpone cheese

1 medium tomato

2 tsp tomato paste

1 tsp chopped fresh chives

1 Using a sharp knife, slice the chicken into fairly thin strips and toss in the flour to coat.

2 Heat the oil in a non-stick skillet and sauté the chicken until golden and thoroughly cooked. Remove the chicken strips from the skillet and drain well on absorbent paper towels.

3 To make the peanut dip, mix together all the ingredients in a bowl (if liked, add a little orange juice to thin the consistency).

4 To make the tomato dip, chop the tomato and mix with the remaining ingredients.

5 Serve the chicken strips with the dips and a selection of vegetable sticks for dipping.

variation

For a refreshing guacamole dip, combine 1 mashed avocado, 2 finely chopped scallions, 1 chopped tomato, 1 finely chopped garlic clove and a squeeze of lemon juice. Remember to add the lemon juice immediately after the avocado has been mashed to prevent discoloration.

variation

For a lower-fat alternative, poach the strips of chicken in a small amount of boiling chicken stock for 6-8 minutes.

chicken with two bell pepper sauce

This quick and simple dish is colorful and healthy. It would be perfect for an impromptu lunch or supper dish.

1

Serves 4

2 tbsp olive oil

2 medium onions, chopped finely

2 garlic cloves, finely chopped

2 red bell peppers, chopped

good pinch cayenne pepper

2 tsp tomato paste

2 yellow bell peppers, chopped

pinch of dried basil

salt and pepper

4 skinless, boneless chicken breasts

⅔ cup dry white wine

⅔ cup chicken stock

bouquet garni

fresh herbs, to garnish

1 Heat 1 tablespoon of oil in each of two medium-sized pans. Place half the chopped onions, 1 of the garlic cloves, the red bell peppers, the cayenne pepper, and the tomato paste in one of the pans. Place the remaining onion, garlic, yellow bell peppers, and basil in the other pan.

3

2 Cover each pan and cook over a very low heat for 1 hour until the bell peppers are soft. If either mixture becomes dry, add a little water. Work each mixture separately in a food processor, then sieve separately.

3 Return the separate mixtures to the pans and season. The two sauces can be gently reheated while the chicken is cooking.

4 Put the chicken breasts into a skillet and add the wine and stock. Add the bouquet garni and bring the liquid to simmer. Cook the chicken for about 20 minutes until tender.

5 To serve, pour a serving of each sauce on to four serving plates, slice the chicken breasts, and arrange on the plates. Garnish with fresh herbs.

4

cook's tip

Make your own bouquet garni by tying together sprigs of your favorite herbs with string, or wrap up dried herbs in a piece of muslin. A popular combination is thyme, parsley, and bay.

spicy peanut chicken

This quick dish has many variations, but this version includes the classic combination of peanuts, chicken, and chiles, blending together to give a wonderfully flavored dish.

Serves 4

10½ oz skinless, boneless chicken breast

2 tbsp peanut oil

1 cup shelled peanuts

1 fresh red chile, sliced

1 green bell pepper, seeded and cut into strips

fried rice, to serve

SAUCE

⅔ cup chicken stock

1 tbsp Chinese rice wine or dry sherry

1 tbsp light soy sauce

1½ tsp light brown sugar

2 garlic cloves, finely chopped

1 tsp grated fresh gingerroot

1 tsp rice-wine vinegar

1 tsp sesame oil

1 Trim any fat from the chicken and cut the meat into 1-inch cubes. Set aside.

2 Heat the peanut oil in a preheated wok. Add the peanuts and stir-fry for 1 minute. Remove the peanuts with a draining spoon and set aside.

3 Add the chicken to the wok and cook for 1–2 minutes. Stir in the chile and green bell pepper and cook for 1 minute. Remove from the wok with a draining spoon and set aside.

4 Put half of the peanuts in a food processor and process until almost smooth. Alternatively, place them in a plastic bag and crush them with a rolling pin.

5 To make the sauce, add the chicken stock, rice wine or dry sherry, soy sauce, sugar, garlic, gingerroot, and rice-wine vinegar to the wok.

6 Heat the sauce without boiling and stir in the peanuts, chicken, chile, and bell pepper.

7 Sprinkle the sesame oil into the wok, stir and cook for 1 minute. Serve hot with fried rice.

cook's tip

If necessary, process the peanuts with a little of the stock in step 4 to form a softer paste.

3

4

6

tom's toad in the hole

This unusual recipe uses chicken and Cumberland sausage, which is then made into individual bite-sized cakes.

Serves 4-6

1 cup all-purpose flour

pinch of salt

1 egg, beaten

1 scant cup milk

¼ cup water

2 tbsp beef drippings

9 oz chicken breasts

9 oz Cumberland sausage

chicken or onion gravy, to serve (optional)

variation

Use skinless, boneless chicken legs instead of chicken breast in the recipe. Cut up as directed. Instead of Cumberland sausage, use your favorite variety of sausage.

1 Mix the flour and salt in a bowl, make a well in the center, and add the beaten egg.

2 Add half the milk, and using a wooden spoon, work in the flour slowly.

2

3

5

3 Beat the mixture until smooth, then add the remaining milk and water.

4 Beat again until the mixture is smooth. Let the mixture stand for at least 1 hour.

5 Add the drippings to individual baking pans or to one large baking pan. Cut up the chicken and sausage so that you get a generous piece in each individual pan or several scattered around the large pan.

6 Heat in a preheated oven, 425°F, for 5 minutes until very hot. Remove the pans from the oven and pour in the batter, leaving space for the mixture to expand.

7 Return to the oven to cook for 35 minutes, until risen and golden brown. Do not open the oven door for at least 30 minutes.

8 Serve while hot, with chicken or onion gravy, or alone.

elizabethan chicken

Chicken is surprisingly delicious when cooked with fruits such as grapes or gooseberries, which make a change from the more usual combinations.

Serves 4

1 tbsp butter

1 tbsp sunflower oil

4 skinless, boneless chicken breasts

4 shallots, finely chopped

¾ cup chicken stock

1 tbsp cider vinegar

1 cup halved seedless grapes

½ cup heavy cream

1 tsp freshly grated nutmeg

salt and pepper

cornstarch, to thicken (optional)

1

variation

If desired, add a little dry white wine or vermouth to the sauce in step 3.

3

4

1 Heat the butter and sunflower oil in a wide, flameproof Dutch oven or pan and quickly sauté the chicken breasts until golden brown, turning once. Remove the chicken and keep warm while you are cooking the shallots.

2 Add the chopped shallots to the pan and sauté gently until softened and lightly browned. Return the chicken breasts to the pan.

3 Add the chicken stock and cider vinegar to the pan, bring to a boil, cover, and simmer gently for 10–12 minutes, stirring occasionally.

4 Transfer the chicken to a serving dish. Add the grapes, cream, and nutmeg to the pan. Heat through, seasoning with salt and pepper to taste. Add a little cornstarch to thicken the sauce, if desired. Pour the sauce over the chicken and serve.

steamed chicken & spring vegetable parcels

A healthy recipe with a delicate Asian flavor, ideal for tender, young, summer vegetables. You'll need large spinach leaves to wrap around the chicken, but make sure they are young leaves.

1

Serves 4

4 boneless, skinless chicken breasts

1 tsp ground lemongrass

salt and pepper

2 scallions, chopped finely

1 cup young carrots

1¼ cups young zucchini

2 stalks celery

1 tsp light soy sauce

¼ cup spinach leaves

2 tsp sesame oil

2

3

1 With a sharp knife, make a slit through one side of each chicken breast, to open out a large pocket. Sprinkle the inside of the pocket with lemongrass, salt, and pepper. Tuck the scallions into the pockets.

2 Trim the carrots, zucchini, and celery and cut into small matchsticks. Plunge them into a pan of boiling water for 1 minute, drain and toss in the soy sauce.

3 Pack the vegetables into the pockets in each chicken breast and fold over firmly to enclose. Reserve any remaining vegetables. Wash the spinach leaves thoroughly, drain, and pat dry with paper towels. Wrap the chicken breasts firmly in the spinach leaves to enclose completely. If the leaves are too firm to wrap the chicken easily, steam them for a few seconds until they are softened and flexible.

4 Place the wrapped chicken in a steamer and steam over rapidly boiling water for 20–25 minutes, depending on size.

5 Stir-fry any leftover vegetable stalks and spinach for 1–2 minutes in the sesame oil and serve with the chicken.

deviled chicken

Chicken is spiked with cayenne pepper and paprika and finished off with a fruity sauce. The sauce is a delicate pink color.

Serves 2-3

¼ cup all-purpose flour

1 tbsp cayenne pepper

1 tsp paprika

12 oz skinless, boneless chicken, diced

2 tbsp butter

1 onion, chopped finely

2 cups milk, warmed

4 tbsp apple purée

¼ cup white grapes

¼ cup sour cream

sprinkle of paprika

1

3

5

1 Mix the flour, cayenne pepper, and paprika together and use to coat the chicken.

2 Shake off any excess flour. Melt the butter in a pan and gently sauté the chicken with the onion for 4 minutes.

3 Stir in the flour and spice mixture. Add the milk slowly, stirring until the sauce thickens.

4 Simmer until the sauce is smooth.

5 Add the apple purée and grapes and simmer gently for 20 minutes.

6 Transfer the chicken and deviled sauce to a serving dish and top with sour cream and a sprinkle of paprika.

cook's tip

Add more paprika if desired — as it is quite a mild spice, you can add plenty without it being too overpowering.

variation

For a healthier alternative to soured cream, use unsweetened yogurt.

mediterranean chicken packets

This method of cooking makes the chicken aromatic and succulent. It also reduces the amount of oil needed since the chicken and vegetables cook in their own juices.

Serves 6

1 tbsp olive oil

6 skinless chicken breast fillets

2 cups mozzarella cheese

3½ cups zucchini, sliced

6 large tomatoes, sliced

pepper

1 small bunch fresh basil or oregano

rice or pasta, to serve

cook's tip

To aid cooking, place the vegetables and chicken on the shiny side of the foil so that once the packet is wrapped up the dull surface of the foil is facing outwards. This ensures that the heat is absorbed into the packet and not reflected away from it.

2

1 Cut six pieces of foil each about 10 inches square. Brush the foil squares lightly with oil and set aside until required.

2 With a sharp knife, slash each chicken breast at intervals, then slice the mozzarella cheese and place between the cuts in the chicken.

3 Divide the zucchini and tomatoes between the pieces of foil and sprinkle with black pepper. Tear or roughly chop the basil or oregano and scatter over the vegetables in each packet.

4 Place the chicken on top of each pile of vegetables then wrap in the foil to enclose the chicken and vegetables, tucking in the ends.

5 Place on a cookie sheet and bake in a preheated oven, 400°F, for about 30 minutes.

6 To serve, unwrap each foil parcel and serve with rice or pasta.

3

4

chicken risotto alla milanese

This famous dish is known throughout the world, and it is perhaps the best known of all Italian risottos, although there are many variations.

Serves 4

⅓ cup butter

2 lb chicken meat, sliced thinly

1 large onion, chopped

2½ cups risotto rice

2½ cups chicken stock

⅓ cup white wine

1 tsp crumbled saffron

salt and pepper

⅓ cup grated Parmesan cheese, to serve

cook's tip

A risotto should have moist but separate grains. Stock should be added a little at a time and only when the last addition has been completely absorbed.

variation

The possibilities for risotto are endless — try adding the following just at the end of cooking time: cashew nuts and corn, lightly sautéed zucchini and basil, or artichokes and oyster mushrooms.

1

2

3

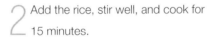

1 Heat 4 tbsp of butter in a deep skillet and sauté the chicken and onion until golden brown.

2 Add the rice, stir well, and cook for 15 minutes.

3 Heat the stock until boiling and gradually add to the rice. Add the white wine, saffron, salt, and pepper to taste and mix well. Simmer gently for 20 minutes, stirring occasionally, and adding more stock if the risotto becomes too dry.

4 Leave to stand for a few minutes and just before serving add a little more stock and simmer for a further 10 minutes. Serve the risotto, sprinkled with the grated Parmesan cheese and the remaining butter.

golden chicken risotto

Ordinary long grain rice can be used instead of risotto rice, but it will not give the traditional, deliciously creamy texture that is typical of Italian risottos.

Serves 4

2 tbsp sunflower oil

1 tbsp butter or margarine

1 medium leek, thinly sliced

1 large yellow bell pepper, diced

3 skinless, boneless chicken breasts, diced

12 oz risotto rice

few strands saffron

salt and pepper

6¼ cups chicken stock

7 oz can corn

¼ cup toasted unsalted peanuts

¼ cup grated Parmesan cheese

cook's tip

Risottos can be frozen, before adding the Parmesan cheese, for up to 1 month, but remember to reheat this risotto thoroughly as it contains chicken.

1 Heat the oil and butter or margarine in a large pan. Sauté the leek and bell pepper for 1 minute then stir in the diced chicken and cook, stirring until golden brown.

1

2 Stir in the rice and cook for 2–3 minutes.

3 Stir in the saffron strands, and salt and pepper to taste. Add the stock, a little at a time, cover and cook over a low heat, stirring occasionally, for about 20 minutes, until the rice is tender and most of the liquid is absorbed. Do not let the risotto dry out – add more stock if necessary.

4 Stir in the corn, peanuts, and Parmesan cheese, then adjust the seasoning to taste. Serve hot.

2

4

speedy peanut pan-fry

A complete main course cooked within ten minutes. Thread egg noodles are the ideal accompaniment because they can be cooked quickly and easily while the stir-fry sizzles.

Serves 4

2 cups zucchini

1½ cups baby corn

3¾ cups white mushrooms

3 cups thread egg noodles

2 tbsp corn oil

1 tbsp sesame oil

8 boneless chicken thighs or 4 breasts,
   sliced thinly

1½ cups beansprouts

4 tbsp smooth peanut butter

2 tbsp soy sauce

2 tbsp lime or lemon juice

½ cup roasted peanuts

pepper

cilantro, to garnish

cook's tip

Try serving this stir-fry with
rice sticks. These are broad,
pale, translucent ribbon
noodles made from ground rice.

1

3

4 Add the beansprouts, peanut
butter, soy sauce, lime or lemon
juice, and pepper, then cook for a further
2 minutes.

5 Drain the noodles, transfer to
a serving dish, scatter with the
peanuts and garnish with cilantro.

4

1 Using a sharp knife, trim and thinly
slice the zucchini, baby corn, and
white mushrooms.

2 Bring a large pan of lightly salted
boiling water to a boil and cook the
noodles for 3–4 minutes. Meanwhile,
heat the corn oil and sesame oil in a
skillet or wok and sauté the chicken over
a fairly high heat for 1 minute.

3 Add the sliced zucchini, baby corn,
and white mushrooms and stir-fry
for 5 minutes.

golden glazed chicken

A glossy glaze with sweet and fruity flavors coats chicken breasts in this tasty recipe.

Serves 6

6 boneless chicken breasts

1 tsp turmeric

1 tbsp whole-grain mustard

1¼ cups orange juice

2 tbsp clear honey

2 tbsp sunflower oil

1½ cups long grain rice

1 orange

3 tbsp chopped mint

mint sprigs, to garnish

1

2

5

variation

To make a slightly sharper sauce, use small grapefruit instead of the oranges.

1 With a sharp knife, mark the surface of the chicken breasts in a diamond pattern. Mix together the turmeric, mustard, orange juice, and honey and pour over the chicken. Chill until required.

2 Lift the chicken from the marinade and pat dry on paper towels.

3 Heat the oil in a wide pan, add the chicken and sauté until golden, turning once. Drain off any excess oil. Pour over the marinade, cover and simmer for 10–15 minutes until the chicken is tender.

4 Boil the rice in lightly salted water until tender and drain well. Finely grate the rind from the orange and stir into the rice with the mint.

5 Using a sharp knife, remove the peel and white pith from the orange and cut the flesh into segments.

6 Serve the chicken with the orange and mint rice, garnished with orange segments and mint sprigs.

chile chicken

This is quite a hot dish, using fresh chiles. If you prefer a milder dish,
halve the number of chiles used.

1

Serves 4

12 oz skinless, boneless lean chicken

½ tsp salt

1 egg white, lightly beaten

2 tbsp cornstarch

4 tbsp vegetable oil

2 garlic cloves, finely chopped

½-inch piece gingerroot, grated

1 red bell pepper, seeded and diced

1 green bell pepper, seeded and diced

2 fresh red chiles, chopped

2 tbsp light soy sauce

1 tbsp dry sherry or Chinese rice wine

1 tbsp wine vinegar

3

1 Cut the chicken into cubes and place in a mixing bowl. Add the salt, egg white, cornstarch, and 1 tablespoon of the oil. Turn the chicken in the mixture to coat thoroughly.

2 Heat the remaining oil in a preheated wok. Add the garlic and gingerroot and stir-fry for 30 seconds.

3 Add the chicken pieces to the wok and stir-fry for 2–3 minutes, or until browned.

4 Stir in the bell peppers, chiles, soy sauce, sherry, or Chinese rice wine, and wine vinegar and cook for a further 2–3 minutes, until the chicken is cooked through. Transfer to a warm serving dish and serve.

4

variation

This recipe also works well if you use 12 oz lean steak, cut into thin strips or 1 lb raw shrimp instead of the chicken.

cook's tip

When preparing chiles, wear rubber gloves to prevent the juices from burning and irritating your hands. Be careful not to touch your face, especially your lips or eyes until you have washed your hands.

lemon chicken

This is on everyone's list of favorite Chinese dishes, and it is so simple to make. It is cooked in minutes and is great served with stir-fried vegetables.

1

Serves 4

vegetable oil, for deep-frying

1½ lb skinless, boneless chicken,

   cut into strips

1 tbsp cornstarch

6 tbsp cold water

3 tbsp fresh lemon juice

2 tbsp sweet sherry

½ tsp superfine sugar

lemon slices and shredded scallion,

   to garnish

1 Heat the oil in a preheated wok until almost smoking. Reduce the heat

3

and stir-fry the chicken strips for 3–4 minutes, until cooked through. Remove the chicken with a draining spoon, set aside and keep warm. Drain the oil from the wok.

2 To make the sauce, mix the cornflour with 2 tablespoons of the water to form a paste.

cook's tip

If you would prefer to use chicken portions rather than strips, cook them in the oil, covered, over a low heat for about 30 minutes, or until cooked through.

3 Pour the lemon juice and remaining water into the mixture in the wok. Add the sherry and sugar and bring to a boil, stirring until the sugar has completely dissolved.

4 Stir in the cornstarch mixture and return to a boil. Reduce the heat and simmer, stirring constantly, for 2-3 minutes, until the sauce is thickened and clear.

5 Transfer the chicken to a warm serving plate and pour the sauce over the top. Garnish with the lemon slices and shredded scallion and serve.

4

poached breast of chicken with whiskey sauce

After cooking with stock and vegetables, chicken breasts are served with a velvety sauce made from whiskey and unsweetened yogurt.

Serves 6

2 tbsp butter

½ cup shredded leeks

⅓ cup diced carrot

¼ cup diced celery

4 shallots, sliced

2½ cups chicken stock

6 chicken breasts

¼ cup whiskey

1 scant cup unsweetened yogurt

2 tbsp freshly grated horseradish

1 tsp honey, warmed

1 tsp chopped fresh parsley

salt and pepper

sprig of fresh parsley, to garnish

1

3

5

1 Melt the butter in a large pan and add the leeks, carrot, celery, and shallots. Cook for 3 minutes, add half the chicken stock, and cook for about 8 minutes.

2 Add the remaining chicken stock, bring to a boil, add the chicken breasts, and cook for 10 minutes.

3 Remove the chicken and thinly slice. Place on a large, hot serving dish and keep warm until required.

4 In another pan, heat the whiskey until reduced by half. Strain the chicken stock through a fine sieve, add to the pan, and reduce the liquid by half.

5 Add the unsweetened yogurt, the horseradish, and the honey. Heat gently and add the chopped parsley and salt and pepper to taste. Stir until well blended.

6 Pour a little of the whiskey sauce around the chicken and pour the remaining sauce into a sauceboat to serve.

7 Serve with a vegetable patty made from the leftover vegetables, mashed potato, and fresh vegetables. Garnish with the parsley sprig.

harlequin chicken

This colorful, simple dish will tempt the appetites of all the family—it is ideal for toddlers, who enjoy the fun shapes of the multi-colored bell peppers.

Serves 4

10 skinless, boneless chicken thighs

1 medium onion

1 each medium red, green, and yellow
  bell peppers

1 tbsp sunflower oil

14 oz can chopped tomatoes

2 tbsp chopped fresh parsley

pepper

whole-wheat bread and a green salad,
  to serve

cook's tip

You can use dried parsley instead of fresh, but remember that you only need about one half of dried to fresh.

1

1 Using a sharp knife, cut the chicken thighs into bite-sized pieces.

2 Peel and thinly slice the onion. Halve and seed the bell peppers and cut into small diamond shapes.

3 Heat the oil in a shallow skillet. Add the chicken and onion and sauté quickly until golden.

2

4 Add the bell peppers, cook for 2–3 minutes, stir in the tomatoes and parsley, and season with pepper.

5 Cover tightly and simmer for about 15 minutes, until the chicken and vegetables are tender. Serve hot with whole-wheat bread and a green salad.

4

cook's tip

If you are making this dish for small children, the chicken can be finely chopped or ground first.

stir-fried turkey with cranberry glaze

This dish encompasses all of the flavors of Thanksgiving with a Chinese theme! Turkey, cranberries, ginger, chestnuts, and soy sauce are blended perfectly.

1

3

cook's tip

If you wish, use a turkey escalope instead of the breast for really tender, lean meat.

cook's tip

It is very important that the wok is very hot before you stir-fry. Test by by holding your hand flat about 3 inches above the base of the interior — you should be able to feel the heat radiating from it.

Serves 2-3

1 turkey breast

2 tbsp sunflower oil

2 tbsp gingerroot

½ cup fresh or frozen cranberries

¼ cup canned chestnuts

4 tbsp cranberry sauce

3 tbsp light soy sauce

salt and pepper

1 Remove any skin from the turkey breast. Using a sharp knife, thinly slice the turkey breast.

2 Heat the oil in a large, preheated wok.

3 Add the turkey to the wok and stir-fry for 5 minutes, or until cooked through.

4 Using a sharp knife, finely chop the gingerroot.

5 Add the gingerroot and the cranberries to the wok and stir-fry for 2–3 minutes or until the cranberries have softened.

6 Add the chestnuts, cranberry sauce, and soy sauce, season to taste with salt and pepper, and allow to bubble for 2–3 minutes.

7 Transfer to warm serving dishes and serve immediately.

4

duck with baby corn & pineapple

The pineapple and plum sauce add a sweetness and fruity flavor to this colorful recipe which blend well with the duck.

Serves 4

4 duck breasts

1 tsp Chinese five-spice powder

1 tbsp cornstarch

1 tbsp chili oil

8 oz baby onions, peeled

2 cloves garlic, finely chopped

1 cup baby corn

1¼ cups canned pineapple chunks

6 scallions, sliced

1 cup beansprouts

2 tbsp plum sauce

1 Remove any skin from the duck breasts. Cut the duck breasts into thin slices.

2 Mix together the five-spice powder and the cornstarch in a large bowl.

3 Toss the duck in the five-spice powder and cornstarch mixture until well coated.

4 Heat the oil in a preheated wok. Stir-fry the duck for 10 minutes, or until just beginning to crisp around the edges.

1

3

4

5 Remove the duck from the wok and set aside until required.

6 Add the onions and garlic to the wok and stir-fry for 5 minutes, or until the onions have softened.

7 Add the baby corn to the wok and stir-fry for a further 5 minutes.

8 Add the pineapple, scallions, and beansprouts and stir-fry for 3–4 minutes. Stir in the plum sauce.

9 Return the cooked duck to the wok and toss until well mixed. Transfer to warm serving dishes and serve hot.

cook's tip

Buy pineapple chunks in natural juice rather than syrup for a fresher flavor. If you can only obtain pineapple in syrup, rinse it in cold water and drain thoroughly before using.

sliced breast of duck with linguine

A raspberry and honey sauce superbly counterbalances the richness of the duck. This exotic dish deserves a special occasion.

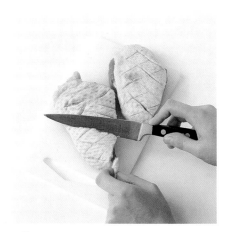

1

Serves 4

10½ oz boned breasts of duck

2 tbsp butter

½ cup finely chopped carrots

4 tbsp finely chopped shallots

1 tbsp lemon juice

½ cup meat stock

4 tbsp honey

¼ cup fresh or thawed frozen raspberries

¼ cup all-purpose flour

salt and pepper

1 tbsp Worcestershire sauce

14 oz fresh linguine

1 tbsp olive oil

fresh raspberries and fresh sprig of flat-leaf
parsley, to garnish

3

1 Trim and score the duck breasts
with a sharp knife and season well
all over. Melt the butter in a skillet, add
the duck breasts, and sauté all over until
lightly colored.

2 Add the carrots, shallots, lemon
juice, and half the meat stock and
simmer over a low heat for 1 minute.
Stir in half the honey and half the
raspberries. Sprinkle over half the flour
and cook, stirring constantly for
3 minutes. Season with pepper and
add the Worcestershire sauce.

3 Stir in the remaining stock and cook
for 1 minute. Stir in the remaining
honey and remaining raspberries and
sprinkle over the remaining flour. Cook
for a further 3 minutes.

6

4 Remove the duck breasts from the
pan, but leave the sauce to continue
simmering over a very low heat.

5 Meanwhile, bring a large pan of
lightly salted water to a boil. Add the
linguine and olive oil and cook until
tender, but still firm to the bite. Drain and
divide between 4 individual plates.

6 Slice the duck breast lengthways
into ¼ inch thick pieces. Pour a little
sauce over the pasta and arrange the
sliced duck in a fan shape on top of it.
Garnish with raspberries and flat-leaf
parsley and serve.

honey-glazed duck

This honey and soy glaze gives a wonderful sheen and flavor to the duck skin. This is such a simple recipe, yet the result is unutterably delicious.

Serves 4

1 tsp dark soy sauce

2 tbsp clear honey

1 tsp garlic vinegar

2 garlic cloves, finely chopped

1 tsp ground star anise

2 tsp cornstarch

2 tsp water

2 large boneless duck breasts, about 8 oz each

celery leaves, cucumber wedges and snipped chives, to garnish

cook's tip

If the duck begins to burn slightly while it is cooking in the oven, cover with foil. Check that the duck breasts are cooked through by inserting the point of a sharp knife into the thickest part of the flesh – the juices should run clear.

2

4

3 Remove the duck from the marinade and cook in a preheated oven, at 425°F for 20–25 minutes, basting frequently with the glaze.

4 Remove the duck from the oven and transfer to a preheated broiler. Broil for about 3–4 minutes to caramelize the top.

5 Remove the duck from the broiler pan and cut into thin slices. Arrange the duck slices in a warm serving dish, garnish with celery leaves, cucumber wedges, and snipped chives, and serve immediately.

5

1 Mix together the soy sauce, clear honey, garlic vinegar, garlic, and star anise. Blend the cornstarch with the water to form a smooth paste and stir it into the mixture.

2 Place the duck breasts in a shallow ovenproof dish. Brush with the soy marinade, turning to coat them completely. Cover and leave to marinate in the refrigerator for at least 2 hours, or overnight if possible.

The wealth of species and flavors that the world's
oceans and rivers provide is immense. Each country
combines its local catch with the region's favorite
herbs and spices to create a variety of dishes.
All of the recipes featured here are easy to prepare
and delicious to eat. Moreover, not only are fish

and seafood quick to cook but they are
also packed full with nutritional
goodness. Naturally low in fat, yet rich
in minerals and proteins, fish and
seafood are important to help balance any
diet. The superb recipes in this chapter

demonstrate the richness of cooking with fish and
seafood. Dishes include modern variations of
traditional recipes, such as Sea Bass in
Olive Sauce on a Bed of Macaroni and Potato-
Topped Cod, and exotic flavors such as
Caribbean Shrimp and Terriyaki Stir-Fried
Salmon with Crispy Leeks.

fish
&
seafood

macaroni & shrimp bake

This adaptation of an eighteenth-century Italian dish is baked until it is golden brown and sizzling, then cut into wedges like a cake.

2

3

3

Serves 4

3 cups dried short-cut macaroni

1 tbsp olive oil, plus extra for brushing

6 tbsp butter, plus extra for greasing

2 small fennel bulbs, thinly sliced and
   fronds reserved

6 oz mushrooms, thinly sliced

6 oz peeled, cooked shrimp

pinch of cayenne pepper

1¼ cups Béchamel sauce
   (see Cook's Tip)

⅔ cup freshly grated Parmesan cheese

2 large tomatoes, sliced

1 tsp dried oregano

salt and pepper

1 Bring a pan of salted water to the boil. Add the pasta and oil and cook until tender, but still firm to the bite. Drain and return to the pan. Add 2 tbsp of butter, cover, shake the pan, and keep warm.

2 Melt the remaining butter in a pan. Sauté the fennel for 3–4 minutes. Stir in the mushrooms and sauté for a further 2 minutes. Stir in the shrimp, then remove the pan from the heat.

3 Stir the cayenne pepper and shrimp mixture into the Béchamel sauce. Pour into a greased ovenproof dish and spread evenly. Sprinkle over the Parmesan cheese and arrange the tomato slices in a ring around the edge. Brush the tomatoes with olive oil and sprinkle over the oregano.

4 Cook in a preheated oven at 350°F for 25 minutes, until golden brown. Serve immediately.

cook's tip

For Béchamel sauce, melt 2 tbsp butter. Stir in ¼ cup flour. Cook, stirring, for 2 minutes. Gradually, stir in 11/4 cups warm milk. Add 2 tbsp finely chopped onion, 5 white peppercorns, and 2 parsley sprigs and season with salt, dried thyme, and grated nutmeg. Simmer, stirring, for 15 minutes. Strain before using.

shrimp with spicy tomatoes

Basil and tomatoes are ideal flavorings for shrimp spiced
with cumin seeds and garlic.

Serves 4

2 tbsp corn oil

1 onion

2 cloves garlic, finely chopped

1 tsp cumin seeds

1 tbsp demerara sugar

14 oz can chopped tomatoes

1 tbsp sun-dried tomato paste

1 tbsp chopped fresh basil

1 lb peeled jumbo shrimp

salt and pepper

cook's tip

Always heat your wok before you
add oil or other ingredients.
This will prevent anything from
sticking to it.

2

4

5

1 Heat the corn oil in a large preheated wok.

2 Using a sharp knife, finely chop the onion.

3 Add the onion and garlic to the wok and stir-fry for 2–3 minutes, or until softened.

4 Stir in the cumin seeds and stir-fry for 1 minute.

5 Add the sugar, chopped tomatoes, and sun-dried tomato paste to the wok. Bring the mixture to the boil, reduce the heat, and leave the sauce to simmer for 10 minutes.

6 Add the basil, shrimp, and salt and pepper to taste to the mixture in the wok. Increase the heat and cook for a further 2–3 minutes or until the shrimp are completely cooked through.

cook's tip

Sun-dried tomato paste has a
much more intense flavor than
that of normal tomato paste. It
adds a distinctive intensity to
any tomato-based dish.

caribbean shrimp

This is an ideal recipe for cooks who have difficulty in finding raw shrimp.

Serves 4

16 cooked tiger shrimp

1 small pineapple

⅔ cup pineapple juice

2 tbsp white wine vinegar

2 tbsp dark muscovado sugar

2 tbsp shredded coconut

flaked coconut, to garnish (optional)

1

2

1 If they are unpeeled, peel the shrimp, leaving the tails attached if preferred.

2 Peel the pineapple and cut it in half lengthwise. Cut one pineapple half into wedges then into chunks.

3 To make the marinade, mix together half of the pineapple juice and the vinegar, sugar, and coconut in a shallow, non-metallic dish. Add the peeled shrimp and pineapple chunks and toss until well coated. Leave the shrimp and pineapple to marinate for at least 30 minutes.

4 Remove the pineapple and shrimp from the marinade and thread them on to skewers. Reserve the marinade.

5 Strain the marinade and place in a food processor. Roughly chop the remaining pineapple and add to the processor with the remaining pineapple juice. Process the pineapple for a few seconds to produce a thick sauce.

6 Pour the sauce into a small pan. Bring to the boil, then simmer for about 5 minutes. This can be done by the side of the grill, if preferred.

7 Transfer the kabobs to the grill and brush with some of the sauce. Grill for about 5 minutes until the kabobs piping hot. Turn the kabobs, brushing occasionally with the sauce. Serve with extra sauce, sprinkled with flaked coconut (if using), on the side.

5

cook's tip

Grill these kabobs just long enough to heat thorough. If cooked for too long, the shrimp will toughen.

shrimp with tomatoes

Quick and easy to prepare, this dish is also extremely good to eat. Use the larger tiger shrimp for special occasions, if you prefer.

1

Serves 4-6

3 medium onions

1 green bell pepper

1 tsp fresh gingerroot, finely chopped

1 tsp fresh garlic, crushed

1 tsp salt

1 tsp chili powder

2 tbsp lemon juice

12 oz frozen shrimp

3 tbsp oil

14 oz can tomatoes

fresh cilantro leaves, to decorate

plain boiled rice and a green salad, to serve

cook's tip

Fresh gingerroot looks rather like a knobbly potato. The skin should be peeled, then the flesh either grated, finely minced, or sliced. Ginger is also available ground: this can be used as a substitute for fresh gingerroot, but the fresh root is far superior.

2

5

1 Using a sharp knife, slice the onions and the green bell pepper.

2 Place the gingerroot, garlic, salt, and chili powder in a small bowl and mix to combine. Add the lemon juice and mix to form a paste.

3 Place the shrimp in a bowl of cold water and set aside to defrost. Drain thoroughly.

4 Heat the oil in a medium-sized pan. Add the onions and sauté until golden brown.

5 Add the spice paste to the onions, reduce the heat to low, and cook, stirring and mixing well, for about 3 minutes.

6 Add the tomatoes and their juice and the green bell pepper, and cook for 5-7 minutes, stirring occasionally.

7 Add the shrimp to the pan and cook for 10 minutes, stirring occasionally. Garnish with fresh cilantro leaves and serve hot with plain boiled rice and a crisp green salad.

stir-fried shrimp with cashew nuts

Cashew nuts are delicious as part of a stir-fry with almost any other ingredient. Use the unsalted variety in cooking.

Serves 4

2 garlic cloves, crushed

1 tbsp cornstarch

pinch of superfine sugar

1 lb raw tiger shrimp

4 tbsp vegetable oil

1 leek, sliced

4½ oz broccoli flowerets

1 orange bell pepper, seeded and diced

¼ cup fish stock

1 tbsp cornstarch

dash of chili sauce

2 tsp sesame oil

1 tbsp Chinese rice wine

¼ cup unsalted cashew nuts

1 Mix together the garlic, cornstarch, and sugar in a bowl. Peel and devein the shrimp. Stir the shrimp into the mixture to coat thoroughly.

2 Heat the oil in a preheated wok and add the shrimp mixture. Stir-fry over a high heat for 20–30 seconds until the shrimp turn pink. Remove the shrimp from the wok with a draining spoon and set aside.

3 Add the leek, broccoli, and bell pepper to the wok and stir-fry for 2 minutes.

4 To make the sauce, mix together the fish stock, cornstarch, chili sauce to taste, the sesame oil, and Chinese rice wine. Add the mixture to the wok, together with the cashew nuts. Return the shrimp to the wok and cook for 1 minute to heat through. Transfer to a warm serving dish and serve immediately.

3

4

variation

This recipe also works well with chicken, pork, or beef strips instead of the shrimp. Use 8 oz meat instead of 1 lb shrimp.

herb & garlic shrimp

Look for raw shrimp in the freezer compartment of large supermarkets or Asian food stores.

Serves 4

12 oz raw shrimp, peeled

2 tbsp chopped, fresh parsley

4 tbsp lemon juice

salt and pepper

2 tbsp olive oil

2¼ oz butter

2 cloves garlic, finely chopped

variation

If raw shrimp are unavailable, use cooked shrimp but reduce the cooking time. Small cooked shrimp can also be cooked in a kitchen foil parcel instead of on the skewers. Marinate and toss the cooked shrimp in the garlic butter, wrap in a kitchen foil, and cook for about 5 minutes, shaking the parcels once or twice.

2

3

1 Place the prepared shrimp in a shallow, non-metallic dish with the parsley, lemon juice, and salt and pepper to taste. Leave the shrimp to marinate in the herb mixture for at least 30 minutes.

2 Heat the oil and butter in a small pan with the garlic until the butter melts. Stir to mix well.

3 Remove the shrimp from the marinade with a draining spoon and add them to the pan containing the garlic butter. Stir the shrimp into the garlic butter until well coated, then thread the shrimp on to skewers.

4 Grill the kabobs over hot coals for 5–10 minutes, turning the skewers occasionally, until the shrimp turn pink and are cooked through. Brush the shrimp with the remaining garlic butter during the cooking time.

4

5 Transfer the herb and garlic shrimp kabobs to serving plates. Drizzle over any of the remaining garlic butter and serve at once.

shrimp omelet

This really is a meal in minutes, combining many Chinese ingredients for a truly tasty dish.

Serves 4

2 tbsp sunflower oil

4 scallions, sliced

12 oz peeled shrimp

1 cup beansprouts

1 tsp cornstarch

1 tbsp light soy sauce

6 eggs

1 Heat the sunflower oil in a large preheated wok.

2 Using a sharp knife, trim the scallions, and cut into slices.

3 Add the shrimp, scallions, and beansprouts to the wok and stir-fry for 2 minutes.

4 Mix together the cornstarch and soy sauce in a small bowl.

2

3

6

cook's tip

It is important to use fresh beansprouts for this dish as the canned ones don't have the crunchy texture necessary.

variation

Add any other vegetables of your choice, such as grated carrot or cooked peas, to the omelet in step 3, if you wish.

5 Beat the eggs with 3 tablespoons of cold water and then blend with the cornstarch and soy mixture.

6 Add the egg mixture to the wok and cook for 5–6 minutes, or until the mixture sets.

7 Transfer the omelet to a serving plate and cut into quarters to serve.

shrimp with bell peppers

This is a colorful and impressive side dish for a dinner party. As there are not many spices in this recipe, use a lot of fresh cilantro in it.

Serves 4

1 lb frozen shrimp

½ bunch fresh cilantro leaves

1 tsp fresh garlic, finely chopped

1 tsp salt

1 medium green bell pepper, sliced

1 medium red bell pepper

5½ tbsp unsalted butter

variation

You could use large tiger shrimp in this dish, if you prefer.

2

4

1 Defrost the shrimp and rinse under cold running water twice. Drain the shrimp thoroughly and place in a large mixing bowl.

2 Using a sharp knife, finely chop the bunch of fresh cilantro.

3 Add the garlic, salt, and fresh cilantro leaves to the shrimp and set aside until required.

4 Seed the bell peppers and cut into thin slices, using a sharp knife.

5 Melt the butter in a large skillet. Add the shrimp to the pan and stir-fry, stirring and tossing the shrimp gently, for 10-12 minutes.

5

6 Add the bell peppers to the pan and cook for a further 3-5 minutes, stirring occasionally.

7 Transfer the shrimp and bell pepper to a serving dish and serve hot.

cantonese shrimp

This shrimp dish is very simple and is ideal for supper or lunch when time is short. It is quite filling because it also contains meat.

1

2

2

Serves 4

5 tbsp vegetable oil

4 garlic cloves, crushed

1½ lb raw shrimp, shelled and deveined

2 inch piece fresh gingerroot,

   finely chopped

6 oz lean pork, diced

1 leek, sliced

2 tbsp dry sherry

2 tbsp light soy sauce

2 tsp superfine sugar

⅔ cup fish stock

4½ tsp cornstarch

3 tbsp water

3 eggs, beaten

shredded leek and red bell pepper

   matchsticks, to garnish

1 Heat 2 tablespoons of the oil in a preheated wok. Add the garlic and stir-fry for 30 seconds. Add the shrimp and stir-fry for 5 minutes, or until they change color. Remove the shrimp from the wok with a draining spoon, set aside, and keep warm.

2 Add the remaining oil to the wok and heat. Add the gingerroot, diced pork, and leek and stir-fry over a medium heat for 4-5 minutes, or until the pork is lightly colored and sealed.

3 Add the sherry, soy sauce, sugar, and fish stock to the wok. Blend the cornstarch with the water to form a smooth paste and stir it into the wok. Cook, stirring, until the sauce thickens and clears.

4 Return the shrimp to the wok and add the beaten eggs. Cook for 5–6 minutes, gently stirring occasionally, until the eggs set. Transfer to a warm serving dish, garnish with shredded leek and bell pepper matchsticks, and serve immediately.

cook's tip

If possible, use Chinese rice wine instead of the sherry.

saffron mussel tagliatelle

Saffron is the most expensive spice in the world, but you only ever need a small quantity. Saffron threads or powdered saffron may be used in this recipe.

Serves 4

2¼ lb mussels

⅔ cup white wine

1 medium onion, finely chopped

2 tbsp butter

2 garlic cloves, crushed

2 tsp cornstarch

1¼ cups heavy cream

pinch of saffron threads or saffron powder

salt and pepper

1 egg yolk

juice of ½ lemon

1 lb dried tagliatelle

1 tbsp olive oil

3 tbsp chopped fresh parsley, to garnish

1 Scrub and debeard the mussels under cold running water. Discard any that do not close when sharply tapped. Put the mussels in a pan with the wine and onion. Cover and cook over a high heat, shaking the pan, for 5–8 minutes, until the shells open.

2 Drain and reserve the cooking liquid. Discard any mussels that are still closed. Reserve a few mussels for the garnish and remove the remainder from their shells.

4

3 Strain the cooking liquid into a pan. Bring to the boil and reduce by about half. Remove the pan from the heat.

4 Melt the butter in a pan. Add the garlic and cook, stirring frequently, for 2 minutes, until golden brown. Stir in the cornstarch and cook, stirring, for 1 minute. Gradually stir in the cooking liquid and the cream. Crush the saffron threads and add to the pan. Season with salt and pepper to taste and simmer over a low heat for 2–3 minutes, until thickened.

5 Stir in the egg yolk, lemon juice, and shelled mussels. Do not allow the mixture to boil.

6 Meanwhile, bring a pan of salted water to the boil. Add the pasta and oil and cook until tender, but still firm to the bite. Drain and transfer to a serving dish. Add the mussel sauce and toss. Garnish with the parsley and reserved mussels and serve.

4

5

mussel casserole

Mussels are not difficult to cook, just a little messy to eat. The flavors are worth it, however, and serving this dish with a finger bowl helps to keep things clean!

Serves 4

2 lb 4 oz mussels

⁄ cup white wine

1 tbsp oil

1 onion, finely chopped

3 garlic cloves, finely chopped

1 red chili, finely chopped

3⁄ oz tomato paste

1 tbsp chopped marjoram

toast or crusty bread, to serve

2

3

4

1 Scrub the mussels to remove any mud or sand.

2 Remove the beards from the mussels by pulling away the hairy bit between the two shells. Rinse the mussels in a bowl of clean water. Discard any mussels that do not close when they are tapped – they are dead and should not be eaten.

3 Place the mussels in a large pan. Pour in the wine and cook for 5 minutes, shaking the pan occasionally until the shells open. Remove and discard any mussels that do not open.

4 Remove the mussels from the pan with a draining spoon. Strain the cooking liquid through a strainer over a bowl, reserving the liquid.

5 Heat the oil in a large skillet. Add the onion, garlic, and chili and cook for 4–5 minutes or until softened.

6 Add the reserved cooking liquid to the pan and cook for 5 minutes or until reduced.

7 Stir in the tomato paste, marjoram, and mussels and cook until hot.

8 Transfer to serving bowls and serve with toast or plenty of crusty bread to mop up the juices.

cook's tip

Finger bowls are individual bowls of warm water with a slice of lemon floating in them. They are used to clean your fingers at the end of a meal.

pasta shells with mussels

Serve this aromatic seafood dish to family and friends who admit to a love of garlic. Offer mints afterwards to freshen the breath.

1

Serves 4-6

2¼ lb mussels

1 cup dry white wine

2 large onions, finely chopped

½ cup unsalted butter

6 large garlic cloves, finely chopped

5 tbsp chopped fresh parsley

1¼ cups heavy cream

salt and pepper

14 oz dried pasta shells

1 tbsp olive oil

crusty bread, to serve

cook's tip

Pasta shells are ideal because the sauce collects in the cavities and impregnates the pasta with flavor.

3

3

1 Scrub and debeard the mussels under cold running water. Discard any that do not close immediately when sharply tapped. Put the mussels into a large pan, together with the wine and half of the onions. Cover and cook over a medium heat, shaking the pan frequently, for 2–3 minutes, until the shells open.

2 Remove the pan from the heat. Drain the mussels and reserve the cooking liquid. Discard any mussels that have not opened. Strain the cooking liquid through a clean cloth into a glass pitcher or bowl and reserve.

3 Melt the butter in a pan over a medium heat. Add the remaining onion and sauté until translucent. Stir in the garlic and cook for 1 minute. Gradually stir in the reserved cooking liquid. Stir in the parsley and cream and season to taste with salt and pepper. Bring to simmering point over a low heat.

4 Meanwhile, bring a large pan of lightly salted water to the boil. Add the pasta and olive oil and cook until just tender, but still firm to the bite. Drain the pasta, return to the pan, cover, and keep warm.

5 Reserve a few mussels for the garnish and remove the remainder from their shells. Stir the shelled mussels into the cream sauce and warm briefly.

6 Transfer the pasta to a large, warm serving dish. Pour over the sauce and toss well to coat. Garnish with the reserved mussels and serve with warm, crusty bread.

spaghetti with seafood sauce

Peeled shrimp from the freezer can become the star ingredient in this colorful and tasty dish. Don't save it for a special occasion!

Serves 4

8 oz dried spaghetti, broken into
   6 inch lengths

2 tbsp olive oil

1 ¼ cups chicken stock

1 tsp lemon juice

1 small cauliflower, cut into flowerets

2 carrots, thinly sliced

4 oz snow peas

4 tbsp butter

1 onion, sliced

8 oz zucchini, sliced

1 garlic clove, finely chopped

12 oz frozen, cooked, peeled shrimp,
   defrosted

salt and pepper

2 tbsp chopped fresh parsley

/ cup freshly grated Parmesan cheese

/ tsp paprika

4 unpeeled, cooked shrimp, to garnish

2

3

4

1 Bring a pan of lightly salted water to the boil. Add the spaghetti and 1 tbsp of the olive oil and cook until tender, but still firm to the bite. Drain the spaghetti and return to the pan. Toss with the remaining olive oil, cover, and keep warm.

2 Bring the chicken stock and lemon juice to the boil. Add the cauliflower and carrots and cook for 3–4 minutes. Remove from the pan and set aside. Add the snow peas to the pan and cook for 1–2 minutes. Set aside with the other vegetables.

3 Melt half the butter in a skillet over a medium heat. Add the onion and zucchini and sauté for about 3 minutes. Add the garlic and shrimp and cook for a further 2–3 minutes, until thoroughly heated through.

4 Stir in the reserved vegetables and heat through. Season to taste with salt and pepper and stir in the remaining butter.

5 Transfer the spaghetti to a warm serving dish. Pour over the sauce and add the chopped parsley. Toss well with 2 forks until coated. Sprinkle over the Parmesan cheese and paprika, garnish with the unpeeled shrimp, and serve immediately.

vermicelli with clams

A quickly cooked recipe that transforms pantry ingredients into a dish with style that is good enough for unexpected guests.

Serves 4

14 oz dried vermicelli, spaghetti or other
   long pasta

2 tbsp olive oil

2 tbsp butter

2 onions, finely chopped

2 garlic cloves, finely chopped

2 x 7 oz jars clams in brine

½ cup white wine

4 tbsp chopped fresh parsley

½ tsp dried oregano

pepper

pinch of freshly grated nutmeg

2 tbsp Parmesan cheese shavings

fresh basil sprigs, to garnish

1 Bring a large pan of lightly salted water to the boil. Add the pasta and half the olive oil and cook until tender, but still firm to the bite. Drain, return to the pan, and add the butter. Cover the pan, shake well and keep warm.

2 Heat the remaining oil in a pan over a medium heat. Add the onions and sauté until they are translucent. Stir in the garlic and cook for 1 minute.

3 Strain the liquid from 1 jar of clams and add the liquid to the pan, with the wine. Stir, bring to simmering point, and simmer for 3 minutes. Drain the second jar of clams and discard the liquid.

4 Add the clams, parsley, and oregano to the pan and season with pepper and nutmeg. Lower the heat and cook until the sauce is heated through.

5 Transfer the pasta to a warm serving dish and pour over the sauce. Sprinkle with the Parmesan cheese, garnish with the basil, and serve immediately.

2

3

4

bacon & scallop skewers

Wrapping bacon around the scallops helps to protect the delicate flesh from the intense heat and allows them to cook without becoming tough. The bacon also imparts a subtle smoky flavor to the scallops.

Makes 4

grated peel and juice of ⁄ lemon

4 tbsp sunflower oil

⁄ tsp dried dill

12 scallops

1 red bell pepper

1 green bell pepper

1 yellow bell pepper

6 strips lean smoked bacon

1 Mix together the lemon peel and juice, oil, and dill in a non-metallic dish. Add the scallops and mix thoroughly to coat in the marinade. Leave to marinate for 1–2 hours.

2 Cut the red, green, and yellow bell peppers in half and seed them. Cut the bell pepper halves into 1 inch pieces and then set aside until required.

3 Carefully remove the peel from the bacon. Stretch the bacon strips with the back of a knife, then cut each bacon strip in half.

4 Remove the scallops from the marinade, reserving any excess marinade. Wrap a piece of bacon around each scallop.

5 Thread the bacon-wrapped scallops on to skewers, alternating with the bell pepper pieces.

6 Grill the bacon and scallop skewers over hot coals for about 5 minutes, basting frequently with the lemon and oil marinade.

7 Transfer the bacon and scallop skewers to serving plates and serve at once.

variation

Peel 4-8 raw shrimp and add them to the marinade with the scallops. Thread them on to the skewers alternately with the scallops and bell peppers.

cook's tip

Hold the skewers with potholders when you are turning them on the grill.

2

3

4

seared scallops with butter sauce

Scallops have a terrific, subtle flavor which is complemented by this buttery sauce pepped up with a hint of chile.

Serves 4

1 lb scallops, without roe

6 scallions

2 tbsp vegetable oil

1 green chile, seeded and sliced

3 tbsp sweet soy sauce

1½ tbsp butter, cubed

1 Rinse the scallops under cold running water, then pat the scallops dry with absorbent paper towels.

2 Using a sharp knife, slice each scallop in half horizontally.

3 Using a sharp knife, trim and slice the scallions.

4 Heat the vegetable oil in a large preheated wok.

2

3

5

5 Add the chile, scallions, and scallops to the wok and stir-fry over a high heat for 4–5 minutes, or until the scallops are just cooked through.

6 Add the soy sauce and butter to the scallop stir-fry and heat through until the butter melts.

7 Transfer to warm serving bowls and serve hot.

cook's tip

If you buy scallops on the shell, slide a knife underneath the membrane to loosen and cut off the tough muscle that holds the scallop to the shell. Discard the black stomach sac and intestinal vein.

cook's tip

Use frozen scallops if preferred, but make sure they are completely defrosted before cooking. In addition, do not overcook them as they will easily disintegrate.

seafood stir-fry

This combination of assorted seafood and tender vegetables delicately flavored with ginger makes an ideal light meal served with thread noodles.

Serves 4

3/ oz small, thin asparagus spears, trimmed

1 tbsp sunflower oil

1 inch piece gingerroot, cut into thin strips

1 medium leek, shredded

2 medium carrots, julienned

3/ oz baby corn, quartered lengthwise

2 tbsp light soy sauce

1 tbsp oyster sauce

1 tsp honey

1 lb cooked, assorted shellfish, thawed
   if frozen

freshly cooked egg noodles, to serve

4 large cooked shrimp and small bunch
   fresh chives, to garnish

1 Bring a small pan of water to the boil and blanch the asparagus for 1–2 minutes. Drain the asparagus, set aside, and keep warm.

2 Heat the oil in a wok or large skillet and stir-fry the gingerroot, leek, carrot, and corn for about 3 minutes.

3 Add the soy sauce, oyster sauce, and honey to the wok or skillet. Stir in the shellfish and continue to stir-fry for 2–3 minutes until the vegetables are just tender and the shellfish are thoroughly heated through. Add the blanched asparagus and stir-fry for about 2 minutes.

4 To serve, pile the cooked noodles on to 4 warm serving plates, and spoon over the seafood and vegetable stir fry. Serve garnished with a large shrimp and freshly snipped chives.

cook's tip

When you are preparing dense vegetables, such as carrots and other root vegetables, for stir-frying, slice them into thin, evenly sized pieces so that they cook quickly and at the same rate. Delicate vegetables, such as bell peppers and scallions, do not need to be cut as thinly.

scallops in ginger sauce

Scallops are both attractive and delicious and make this a special dish.
Cooked with ginger and orange, this dish is perfect served with plain rice.

1

Serves 4

2 tbsp vegetable oil

1 lb scallops, cleaned and halved

1-inch piece fresh gingerroot,
   finely chopped

3 garlic cloves, crushed

2 leeks, shredded

¼ cup shelled English peas

4½ oz canned bamboo shoots,
   drained and rinsed

2 tbsp light soy sauce

2 tbsp unsweetened orange juice

1 tsp superfine sugar

orange zest, to garnish

cook's tip

The edible parts of a
scallop are the round white
muscle and the orange and
white coral or roe. The frilly
skirt surrounding the muscle —
the gills and mantle — may
be used for making shellfish
stock. All other parts should
be discarded.

2

3

1 Heat the oil in a preheated wok. Add the scallops and stir-fry for 1–2 minutes. Remove the scallops from the wok with a draining spoon and set aside.

2 Add the gingerroot and garlic to the wok and stir-fry for 30 seconds. Stir in the leeks and peas and cook, stirring, for a further 2 minutes.

3 Add the bamboo shoots and return the scallops to the wok. Stir gently to mix without breaking up the scallops.

4 Stir in the soy sauce, orange juice, and sugar and cook for 1–2 minutes. Transfer to a serving dish, garnish with the orange zest, and serve immediately.

cook's tip

Frozen scallops may be thawed
and used in this recipe, adding
them at the end of cooking to
prevent them from breaking up.
If you are buying scallops
already shelled, check whether
they are fresh or frozen. Fresh
scallops are cream colored and
more translucent, while frozen
scallops tend to be pure white.

crab in ginger sauce

In this recipe, the crabs are served in the shell for ease and visual effect and coated in a glossy ginger sauce.

2

Serves 4

2 small cooked crabs

2 tbsp vegetable oil

3 inch piece fresh gingerroot, grated

2 garlic cloves, thinly sliced

1 green bell pepper, seeded and cut into
   thin strips

6 scallions, cut into 1 inch lengths

2 tbsp dry sherry

½ tsp sesame oil

⅔ cup fish stock

1 tsp light brown sugar

2 tsp cornstarch

⅔ cup water

1 Rinse the crabs and gently loosen around the shell at the top. Using a sharp knife, cut away the grey tissue and discard. Rinse the crabs again.

2 Twist off the legs and claws from the crabs. Using a pair of crab claw crackers or a cleaver, gently crack the claws to break through the shell to expose the flesh. Remove and discard any loose pieces of shell.

3 Separate the body and discard the inedible lungs and sac. Cut down the center of each crab to separate the body into two pieces and then cut each of these in half again.

4 Heat the oil in a preheated wok. Add the gingerroot and garlic and stir-fry for 1 minute. Add the crab pieces and stir-fry for 1 minute.

5 Stir in the bell pepper, scallions, sherry, sesame oil, stock, and sugar. Bring to the boil, reduce the heat, cover and simmer for 3–4 minutes.

6 Blend the cornstarch with the remaining water and stir it into the wok. Bring to the boil, stirring, until the sauce is thickened and clear. Transfer to a warm serving dish and serve immediately.

cook's tip

If preferred, remove the crabmeat from the shells prior to stir-frying and add to the wok with the bell pepper.

2

3

stir-fried squid with green bell peppers & black bean sauce

Contrary to popular belief squid is not tough and rubbery, unless it is overcooked.

Serves 4

1 lb squid rings

2 tbsp all-purpose flour

½ tsp salt

1 green bell pepper

2 tbsp peanut oil

1 red onion, sliced

5½ oz jar black bean sauce

1 Rinse the squid rings under cold running water and pat dry with paper towels.

2 Place the all-purpose flour and salt in a bowl and mix together. Add the squid rings and toss until they are finely coated.

2

3

3 Using a sharp knife, seed the bell pepper. Slice the bell pepper into thin strips.

4 Heat the peanut oil in a large preheated wok.

5 Add the bell pepper and red onion to the wok and stir-fry for about 2 minutes, or until the vegetables are just beginning to soften.

6 Add the squid rings to the wok and cook for a further 5 minutes, or until the squid is cooked through.

7 Add the black bean sauce to the wok and heat through until the juices are bubbling. Transfer to warm serving bowls and serve immediately.

5

cook's tip

Serve this recipe with fried rice or noodles tossed in soy sauce, if you wish.

citrus fish skewers

You can use your favorite fish for this dish as long as it is firm enough to thread on to a skewer. The tang of orange makes this a refreshing light meal.

Serves 4

1 lb firm white fish fillets (such as cod or
   angler fish)

1 lb thick salmon fillet

2 large oranges

1 pink grapefruit

1 bunch fresh bay leaves

1 tsp finely grated lemon peel

3 tbsp lemon juice

2 tsp honey

2 garlic cloves, finely chopped

salt and pepper

crusty bread and mixed salad, to serve

1 Skin the white fish and the salmon, rinse, and pat dry on absorbent paper towels. Cut each fillet into 16 pieces.

2 Using a sharp knife, remove the skin and pith from the oranges and grapefruit. Cut out the segments of flesh, removing all remaining traces of the pith and dividing membrane.

3 Thread the pieces of fish alternately with the orange and grapefruit segments and the bay leaves on to 8 skewers. Place the skewers in a shallow dish.

4 Mix together the lemon peel and juice, the honey, and garlic. Pour over the fish skewers and season well. Cover and chill for 2 hours, turning occasionally.

5 Preheat the broiler to medium. Remove the skewers from the marinade and place on the rack. Cook for 7–8 minutes, turning once, until cooked through.

6 Drain, transfer to serving plates, and serve with crusty bread and a mixed salad.

variation

This dish makes an unusual appetizer. Try it with any firm fish — swordfish or shark, for example — or with tuna for a meatier texture.

1

2

3

potato-topped cod

This simple dish has a spicy bread crumb mixture topping layers of cod and potatoes. It is cooked in the oven until crisp and golden.

Serves 4

¼ cup butter

4 waxy potatoes, sliced

1 large onion, finely chopped

1 tsp whole-grain mustard

1 tsp garam masala

pinch of chili powder

1 tbsp chopped fresh dill

1¼ cups fresh bread crumbs

4 cod fillets, about 6 oz each

salt and pepper

1¼ oz Gruyère cheese, grated

fresh dill sprigs, to garnish

2

3

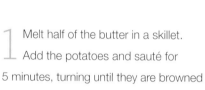

4

1 Melt half of the butter in a skillet. Add the potatoes and sauté for 5 minutes, turning until they are browned all over. Remove the potatoes from the pan with a draining spoon.

2 Add the remaining butter to the skillet and stir in the onion, mustard, garam masala, chili powder, chopped dill, and bread crumbs. Cook for 1-2 minutes, stirring and mixing well.

3 Layer half of the potatoes in the base of an ovenproof dish and place the cod fillets on top. Cover the cod fillets with the rest of the potato slices. Season to taste with salt and pepper.

4 Spoon the spicy mixture from the skillet over the potato and sprinkle with the grated cheese.

5 Cook in a preheated oven at 400°F for 20-25 minutes or until the topping is golden and crisp and the fish is cooked through. Garnish with fresh dill sprigs and serve at once.

stir-fried fish with coconut & basil

Fish curries are sensational and this Thai curry is no exception. Red curry and coconut are fantastic flavors with the fried fish.

3

Serves 4

2 tbsp vegetable oil

1 lb skinless cod fillet

¼ cup seasoned flour

1 clove garlic, finely chopped

2 tbsp red Thai curry paste

1 tbsp fish sauce (nam pla)

1¼ cups coconut milk

6 oz cherry tomatoes, halved

20 fresh basil leaves

fragrant rice, to serve

1 Heat the vegetable oil in a large preheated wok.

2 Using a sharp knife, cut the fish into large cubes, taking care to remove any bones with a pair of tweezers.

3 Place the seasoned flour in a bowl. Add the cubes of fish and mix until well coated.

4

5

4 Add the coated fish to the wok and stir-fry over a high heat for 3–4 minutes, or until the fish just begins to brown at the edges.

5 Mix together the garlic, curry paste, fish sauce, and coconut milk in a bowl. Pour the mixture over the fish and bring to the boil.

6 Add the tomatoes to the mixture in the wok and leave to simmer for 5 minutes.

7 Roughly chop or tear the fresh basil leaves. Add the basil to the wok, stir carefully to combine, taking care not to break up the cubes of fish.

8 Transfer to serving plates and serve hot with fragrant rice.

cook's tip

Take care not to overcook the dish once the tomatoes are added, otherwise they break down and the skins come away.

fresh-baked sardines

Here, fresh sardines are baked with eggs, herbs, and vegetables to form a dish similar to an omelet.

2

Serves 4

2 tbsp olive oil

2 large onions, sliced into rings

3 garlic cloves, finely chopped

2 large zucchini, cut into sticks

3 tbsp fresh thyme, stalks removed

8 sardine fillets or about 2 lb 4 oz whole
     sardines, filleted

2¼ oz Parmesan cheese, grated

4 eggs, beaten

⅓ pint milk

salt and pepper

4

4

variation

If you cannot find sardines
that are large enough to
fillet, small mackerel could
be used instead.

1 Heat 1 tablespoon of the oil in a
skillet. Add the onions and garlic
and sauté for 2–3 minutes.

2 Add the zucchini to the skillet
and cook for about 5 minutes or
until golden.

3 Stir 2 tablespoons of the thyme into
the mixture.

4 Place half of the onions and
zucchini in the base of a large
ovenproof dish. Top with the sardine
fillets and half of the Parmesan cheese.

5 Place the remaining onions and
zucchini on top and sprinkle with
the remaining thyme.

6 Mix the eggs and milk together in a
bowl and season to taste with salt
and pepper. Pour the mixture over the
vegetables and sardines in the dish.
Sprinkle the remaining Parmesan cheese
over the top.

7 Bake in a preheated oven at
350°F for 20–25 minutes or until
golden and set. Serve hot, straight from
the oven.

stir-fried cod with mango

Fish and fruit are a classic combination, and in this recipe a tropical flavor is added which gives a great scented taste to the dish.

Serves 4

6 oz carrots

2 tbsp vegetable oil

1 red onion, sliced

1 red bell pepper, seeded and sliced

1 green bell pepper, seeded and sliced

1 lb skinless cod fillet

1 ripe mango

1 tsp cornstarch

1 tbsp soy sauce

1¼ cup tropical fruit juice

1 tbsp lime juice

1 tbsp chopped cilantro

variation

You can use papaya as an alternative to the mango, if you prefer.

1

5

1 Using a sharp knife, slice the carrots into thin sticks.

2 Heat the vegetable oil in a preheated wok.

3 Add the onion, carrots, and bell peppers to the wok and stir-fry for 5 minutes.

4 Using a sharp knife, cut the cod into small cubes.

5 Peel the mango, then carefully remove the flesh from the center stone. Cut the flesh into thin slices.

6 Add the cod and mango to the wok and stir-fry for a further 4–5 minutes, or until the fish is cooked through. Do not stir the mixture too much or you may break the fish up.

7 Mix the cornstarch, soy sauce, fruit juice, and lime juice in a small bowl.

8 Pour the cornstarch mixture over the stir-fry and allow the mixture to bubble and the juices to thicken. Scatter with cilantro and serve immediately.

7

celery & salt cod casserole

Salt cod is dried and salted in order to preserve it. It has an unusual flavor, which goes particularly well with celery in this dish.

Serves 4

9 oz salt cod, soaked overnight

1 tbsp oil

4 shallots, finely chopped

2 garlic cloves, finely chopped

3 celery stalks, chopped

1 x 14 oz can tomatoes, chopped

⅔ cup fish stock

1¼ oz pine nuts

2 tbsp roughly chopped tarragon

2 tbsp capers

crusty bread or mashed potato, to serve

cook's tip

Salt cod is a useful ingredient to keep in the pantry and once soaked, can be used in the same way as any other fish. It does, however, have a stronger flavor than normal, and it is slightly salty. It can be found in fish stores, larger stores, and delicatessens.

1

2

1 Drain the salt cod, rinse it under plenty of running water, and drain again thoroughly. Remove and discard any skin and bones. Pat the fish dry with paper towels and cut it into chunks.

2 Heat the oil in a large skillet. Finely chop the shallots and garlic, add to the skillet, and sauté for 2–3 minutes. Add the celery, cook for a further 2 minutes, and add the tomatoes and stock.

3 Bring the mixture to the boil, reduce the heat, and leave to simmer for 5 minutes.

4 Add the fish and cook for 10 minutes or until tender.

5 Meanwhile, place the pine nuts on a cookie sheet. Place under a preheated broiler and broil for 2–3 minutes or until golden.

6 Stir the tarragon, capers, and pine nuts into the fish casserole and heat gently to warm through.

7 Transfer to serving plates and serve with fresh crusty bread or mashed potato.

5

marinated fish

Marinating fish, for even a short period, adds a subtle flavor to the flesh and makes even simply broiled or fried fish a delicious dish.

2

3

4

cook's tip

If the lime is too hard to squeeze, microwave on high power for 30 seconds to release the juice. This dish is also excellent cooked on the grill.

Serves 4

4 whole mackerel, cleaned and gutted
4 tbsp chopped marjoram
2 tbsp extra virgin olive oil
finely grated peel and juice of 1 lime
2 garlic cloves, finely chopped
salt and pepper

1 Under gently running water, scrape the mackerel with the blunt side of a knife to remove any scales.

2 Using a sharp knife, make a slit in the stomach of the fish and cut horizontally along until the knife will go no further very easily. Gut the fish and rinse under water. You may prefer to remove the heads before cooking, but it is not necessary.

3 Using a sharp knife, cut 4–5 diagonal slashes on each side of the fish. Place the fish in a shallow, nonmetallic dish.

4 To make the marinade, mix together the marjoram, olive oil, lime peel and juice, garlic, and salt and pepper in a bowl.

5 Pour the mixture over the fish. Leave to marinate in the refrigerator for 30 minutes.

6 Cook the mackerel, under a preheated broiler, for 5–6 minutes on each side, brushing occasionally with the reserved marinade, until golden.

7 Transfer the fish to serving plates. Pour over any remaining marinade before serving.

salt cod fritters

These tasty little fried cakes of mashed salt cod mixed with fennel and a little chile make an excellent snack or main course served with vegetables and a chili relish.

Makes 28 cakes

3½ oz self-rising flour

1 egg, beaten

⅔ cup milk

9 oz salt cod, soaked overnight

1 small red onion, finely chopped

1 small fennel bulb, finely chopped

1 red chile, finely chopped

2 tbsp oil

crisp salad and chili relish, or cooked rice
   and fresh vegetables, to serve

cook's tip

If you prefer larger fritters,
use 2 tbsp per fritter and
cook for slightly longer.

2

5

5

1 Sift the flour into a large bowl. Make a well in the center of the flour and add the egg.

2 Using a wooden spoon, gradually draw in the flour, slowly adding the milk, and mix to form a smooth batter. Leave to stand for 10 minutes.

3 Drain the salt cod and rinse it under cold running water. Drain again thoroughly.

4 Remove and discard the skin and any bones from the fish, then mash the flesh with a fork.

5 Place the fish in a large bowl and combine with the onion, fennel, and chile. Add the mixture to the batter and blend together.

6 Heat the oil in a large skillet and, taking about 1 tablespoon of the mixture at a time, spoon it into the hot oil. Cook the fritters, in batches, for 3–4 minutes on each side until golden and slightly puffed. Keep warm while cooking the remaining mixture.

7 Serve with salad and a chili relish for a light meal or with vegetables and rice.

herrings with hot pesto sauce

By making a simple pesto sauce, but omitting the cheese, it is possible to heat the paste without it becoming stringy, so it can be used as a hot sauce.

Serves 4

4 whole herrings or small mackerel, cleaned and gutted

2 tbsp olive oil

8 oz tomatoes, peeled, seeded and chopped

8 canned anchovy fillets, chopped

about 30 fresh basil leaves

1¼ oz pine nuts

2 garlic cloves, finely chopped

cook's tip

Try grilling the fish for an extra char-grilled flavor, if you prefer.

3

4

5

1 Cook the herrings under a preheated broiler for about 8-10 minutes on each side, or until the skin is slightly charred on both sides.

2 Meanwhile, heat 1 tablespoon of the olive oil in a large pan.

3 Add the tomatoes and anchovies to the pan and cook over a medium heat for 5 minutes.

4 Meanwhile, place the basil, pine nuts, garlic, and remaining oil into a food processor and blend to form a smooth paste. Alternatively, pound ingredients by hand in a mortar and pestle.

5 Add the pesto mixture to the pan containing the tomato and anchovy mixture and stir to heat through.

6 Spoon some of the pesto sauce on to warm individual serving plates. Place the fish on top and pour the rest of the pesto sauce over the fish. Serve immediately.

steamed fish with black bean sauce

The Chinese use a lot of whole fish in their cooking, and steaming is one of their preferred methods. It helps maintain both the flavor and the texture.

1

Serves 4

2 lb whole snapper, cleaned and scaled

3 garlic cloves, crushed

2 tbsp black bean sauce

1 tsp cornstarch

2 tsp sesame oil

2 tbsp light soy sauce

2 tsp superfine sugar

2 tbsp dry sherry

1 small leek, shredded

1 small red bell pepper, seeded and cut into
    thin strips

shredded leek and lemon wedges,
    to garnish

boiled rice or noodles, to serve

2

1 Rinse the fish inside and out with cold running water and pat dry with paper towels. Make 2-3 diagonal slashes in the flesh on each side of the fish, using a sharp knife. Rub the garlic into the fish.

2 Thoroughly mix the black bean sauce, cornstarch, sesame oil, light soy sauce, sugar, and dry sherry together in a bowl. Place the fish in a shallow heatproof dish and pour the sauce mixture over the top.

3 Sprinkle the leek and bell pepper strips on top of the sauce. Place the dish in the top of a steamer, cover, and steam for 10 minutes, or until the fish is cooked through. Transfer to a serving dish, garnish with shredded leek and lemon wedges, and serve with boiled rice or noodles.

cook's tip

Insert the point of a sharp knife into the fish to test if it is cooked. The fish is cooked through if the knife goes into the flesh easily.

variation

Whole sea bream or sea bass may be used instead of snapper, if you prefer.

3

poached salmon steaks with lemon & watercress sauce

Fresh salmon and pasta in a mouthwatering lemon and watercress sauce makes a wonderful summer evening treat.

Serves 4

4 x 10 oz fresh salmon steaks

4 tbsp butter

¼ cup dry white wine

sea salt

8 peppercorns

fresh dill sprig

fresh tarragon sprig

1 lemon, sliced

1 lb dried penne

2 tbsp olive oil

lemon slices and fresh watercress,
   to garnish

LEMON & WATERCRESS SAUCE

2 tbsp butter

¼ cup all-purpose flour

⅞ cup warm milk

juice and finely grated peel of 2 lemons

2 oz watercress, chopped

salt and pepper

1

4

5

1 Put the salmon in a large, non-stick pan. Add the butter, wine, a pinch of sea salt, the peppercorns, dill, tarragon, and lemon. Cover, bring to the boil, and simmer for 10 minutes.

2 Using a fish slice, carefully remove the salmon. Strain and reserve the cooking liquid. Remove and discard the salmon skin and center bones. Place on a warm dish, cover, and keep warm.

3 Meanwhile, bring a pan of salted water to the boil. Add the penne and 1 tablespoon of the oil and cook for 12 minutes until tender but still firm to the bite. Drain and sprinkle over the remaining olive oil. Place on a warm serving dish, top with the salmon steaks, and keep warm.

4 To make the sauce, melt the butter and stir in the flour for 2 minutes. Stir in the milk and about 7 tablespoons of the reserved cooking liquid. Add the lemon juice and peel and cook, stirring, for a further 10 minutes.

5 Add the watercress to the sauce, stir gently, and season to taste with salt and pepper.

6 Pour the sauce over the salmon, garnish with slices of lemon and fresh watercress, and serve immediately.

five-spice salmon with ginger stir-fry

Five-spice powder is a fragrant blend of star anise, fennel, cinnamon, cloves, and Szechuan peppercorns that is often used in Chinese dishes.

Serves 4

4 salmon fillets, skinned, 4 oz each

2 tsp five-spice powder

pepper

1 large leek

1 large carrot

4 oz snow peas

1 inch piece gingerroot

2 tbsp ginger wine

2 tbsp light soy sauce

1 tbsp vegetable oil

shredded leek, gingerroot and carrot,
   to garnish

freshly boiled noodles, to serve

1

2

3

1 Wash the salmon and pat dry on absorbent paper towels. Rub the five-spice powder into both sides of the fish and season with freshly ground pepper. Set aside until required.

2 Trim the leek, slice it down the center, and rinse under cold water to remove any dirt. Finely shred the leek. Peel the carrot and cut it into very thin strips. Top and tail the snow peas and cut them into shreds. Peel the gingerroot and slice thinly into strips.

3 Place all of the vegetables into a large bowl and toss in the ginger wine and 1 tbsp soy sauce. Set aside.

4 Preheat the broiler to medium. Place the salmon fillets on the rack and brush with the remaining soy sauce. Cook for 2–3 minutes on each side until cooked through.

5 While the salmon is cooking, heat the oil in a non-stick wok or large skillet and stir-fry the vegetables for 5 minutes until just tender. Take care not to overcook the vegetables—they should still have bite. Transfer to serving plates.

6 Drain the salmon on absorbent paper towels and serve on a bed of stir-fried vegetables. Garnish with shredded leek, gingerroot, and carrot and serve with noodles.

stir-fried salmon with pineapple

Presentation plays a major part in Chinese cooking and this dish demonstrates this perfectly with the wonderful combination of colors.

Serves 4

1 cup baby corn

2 tbsp sunflower oil

1 red onion, sliced

1 orange bell pepper, seeded and sliced

1 green bell pepper, seeded and sliced

1 lb salmon fillet, skin removed

1 tbsp paprika

8 oz can cubed pineapple, drained

1 cup beansprouts

2 tbsp tomato catsup

2 tbsp soy sauce

2 tbsp medium sherry

1 tsp cornstarch

variation

You can use trout fillets instead of the salmon as an alternative, if you prefer.

1

2

4

1 Using a sharp knife, cut the baby corn in half.

2 Heat the sunflower oil in a large preheated wok. Add the onion, bell peppers, and baby corn to the wok and stir-fry for 5 minutes.

3 Rinse the salmon fillet under cold running water and pat dry with absorbent paper towels.

4 Cut the salmon flesh into thin strips and place in a large bowl. Sprinkle with the paprika and toss until well coated.

5 Add the salmon to the wok together with the pineapple and stir-fry for a further 2–3 minutes or until the fish is tender.

6 Add the beansprouts to the wok and toss well.

7 Mix together the tomato catsup, soy sauce, sherry and cornstarch. Add the mixture to the wok and cook until the juices start to thicken. Transfer to warm serving plates and serve immediately.

spaghetti with smoked salmon

Made in moments, this is a luxurious dish to astonish and delight unexpected guests. It is very rich so a little goes a long way.

2

Serves 4

1 lb dried buckwheat spaghetti

2 tbsp olive oil

1¼ cups heavy cream

¼ cup whiskey or brandy

4½ oz smoked salmon

pinch of cayenne pepper

pepper

2 tbsp chopped fresh cilantro or parsley

½ cup crumbled feta cheese

fresh cilantro or parsley leaves, to garnish

3

3

1 Bring a large pan of lightly salted water to the boil. Add the spaghetti and 1 tablespoon of the olive oil and cook until tender, but still firm to the bite. Drain the spaghetti, return to the pan, and sprinkle over the remaining olive oil. Cover, shake the pan, set aside, and keep warm.

2 Pour the cream into a small pan and bring to simmering point, but do not let it boil. Pour the whiskey or brandy into another small pan and bring to simmering point, but do not allow it to boil. Remove both pans from the heat and mix together the cream and whiskey or brandy.

3 Cut the smoked salmon into thin strips and add to the cream mixture. Season to taste with cayenne and pepper. Just before serving, stir in the chopped fresh cilantro or parsley.

4 Transfer the spaghetti to a warm serving dish, pour over the sauce, and toss thoroughly with 2 large forks. Scatter over the crumbled feta cheese, garnish with the cilantro or parsley leaves, and serve immediately.

cook's tip

Serve this rich and luxurious dish with a green salad tossed in a lemony dressing.

teriyaki stir-fried salmon with crispy leeks

Teriyaki is a wonderful Japanese dish which is delicious when made with salmon and served on a bed of crispy leeks.

Serves 4

1 lb salmon fillet, skinned

2 tbsp sweet soy sauce

2 tbsp tomato catsup

1 tsp rice-wine vinegar

1 tbsp light brown sugar

1 clove garlic, crushed

4 tbsp corn oil

1 lb leeks, thinly shredded

finely chopped red chiles, to garnish

variation

You can use a tenderloin of beef instead of the salmon, if you prefer.

1

3

5

1 Using a sharp knife, cut the salmon into slices. Place the slices of salmon in a shallow, non-metallic dish.

2 Mix together the soy sauce, tomato catsup, rice-wine vinegar, sugar, and garlic.

3 Pour the mixture over the salmon, toss well, and leave to marinate for about 30 minutes.

4 Meanwhile, heat 3 tablespoons of the corn oil in a large preheated wok.

5 Add the leeks to the wok and stir-fry over a medium high heat for about 10 minutes, or until the leeks become crispy and tender.

6 Using a draining spoon, carefully remove the leeks from the wok and transfer to warmed serving plates.

7 Add the remaining oil to the wok. Add the salmon and the marinade to the wok and cook for 2 minutes. Spoon over the leeks, garnish with red chiles, and serve immediately.

sweet & sour fish salad

This refreshing blend of pink and white fishes mixed with fresh pineapple and bell peppers makes an interesting appetizer or a light meal.

Serves 4

8 oz trout fillets

8 oz white fish fillets (such as haddock
   or cod)

1¼ cups water

1 stalk lemongrass

2 lime leaves

1 large red chile

1 bunch scallions, trimmed and shredded

4 oz fresh pineapple flesh, diced

1 small red bell pepper, seeded and diced

1 bunch watercress, washed and trimmed

fresh snipped chives, to garnish

DRESSING

1 tbsp sunflower oil

1 tbsp rice-wine vinegar

pinch of chili powder

1 tsp honey

salt and pepper

1

2

1 Rinse the fish, place in a skillet,
and pour over the water. Bend the
lemongrass in half to bruise it and add
to the pan with the lime leaves. Prick
the chile with a fork and add to the pan.
Bring to the boil and simmer for
7–8 minutes. Let cool.

2 Drain the fish fillet, flake the flesh
away from the skin, and place
in a bowl. Gently stir in the scallions,
pineapple, and bell pepper.

3

3 Arrange the washed watercress
on 4 serving plates, pile the cooked
fish mixture on top, and set aside.

4 To make the dressing, mix all the
ingredients together and season
well. Spoon over the fish and serve
garnished with chives.

variation

This recipe also works
very well if you replace the
fish with 12 oz white crab
meat. Add a dash of Tabasco
sauce if you like it hot!

sole fillets in marsala & cream

A rich wine and cream sauce makes this an excellent dinner party dish. You can make the stock the day before so it takes only minutes to cook and serve the fish.

Serves 4

2½ cups water

bones and skin from the sole fillets

1 onion, peeled and halved

1 carrot, peeled and halved

3 fresh bay leaves

SAUCE

1 tbsp olive oil

1 tbsp butter

4 shallots, finely chopped

3½ oz baby white mushrooms,
    wiped and halved

1 tbsp peppercorns, lightly crushed

8 sole fillets

⅓ cup Marsala

⅔ pint heavy cream

cooked vegetables, to serve

1

1 To make the stock, place the water, fish bones and skin, onion, carrot, and bay leaves in a pan and bring to a boil.

2 Reduce the heat and leave the mixture to simmer for 1 hour or until the stock has reduced to about ⅔ cup. Drain the stock through a fine strainer, discarding the bones and vegetables, and set aside.

3 To make the sauce, heat the oil and butter in a skillet. Add the shallots, and cook, stirring, for 2–3 minutes or until just softened.

4 Add the mushrooms to the skillet and cook, stirring, for a further 2–3 minutes or until they are just beginning to brown.

5 Add the peppercorns and sole fillets to the skillet. Cook the sole fillets for 3–4 minutes on each side or until golden brown.

6 Pour the wine and stock over the fish and leave to simmer for 3 minutes. Remove the fish with a fish slice or a draining spoon, set aside, and keep warm.

4

5

7 Increase the heat and boil the mixture in the pan for about 5 minutes or until the sauce has reduced and thickened.

8 Pour in the cream, return the fish to the pan, and heat through. Serve with the cooked vegetables of your choice.

vermicelli with fillets of red mullet

This simple recipe perfectly complements the sweet flavor and delicate texture of the fish.

Serves 4

2¼ lb red mullet fillets

1¼ cups dry white wine

4 shallots, finely chopped

1 garlic clove, finely chopped

3 tbsp finely chopped mixed fresh herbs

finely grated peel and juice of 1 lemon

pinch of freshly grated nutmeg

3 anchovy fillets, roughly chopped

salt and pepper

2 tbsp heavy cream

1 tsp cornstarch

1 lb dried vermicelli

1 tbsp olive oil

1 fresh mint sprig, lemon slices, and
    lemon rind, to garnish

cook's tip

The best red mullet is
sometimes called golden
mullet, although it is
bright red in color.

1

2

3

1 Put the red mullet fillets in a large Dutch oven. Pour over the wine and add the shallots, garlic, chopped herbs, lemon peel and juice, nutmeg, and anchovies. Season to taste with salt and pepper. Cover and bake in a preheated oven at 350°F for 35 minutes.

2 Carefully transfer the mullet to a warm dish. Set aside and keep warm while you prepare the sauce and pasta.

3 Pour the cooking liquid into a pan and bring to the boil. Simmer for 25 minutes or until reduced by half. Mix together the cream and cornstarch and stir into the sauce to thicken.

4 Meanwhile, bring a large pan of lightly salted water to the boil. Add the vermicelli and olive oil and cook for 8–10 minutes, until tender, but still firm to the bite. Drain the pasta and transfer to a warm serving dish.

5 Arrange the red mullet fillets on top of the vermicelli and pour over the sauce. Garnish with a fresh mint sprig, slices of lemon and strips of lemon rind, and serve immediately.

steamed mullet & piquant sauce

Ginger is widely used in Chinese cooking for its strong, pungent flavour. Always use fresh gingerroot wherever possible, although ground can also be used.

2

3

4 Place the vinegar, soy sauce, sugar, chili sauce, fish stock, bell pepper, and tomato in a pan and bring to the boil, stirring occasionally. Cook over a high heat until the sauce has reduced slightly and thickened.

5 Remove the fish from the steamer and transfer to a warm serving dish. Pour the sauce over the fish, garnish with tomato slices and serve at once.

Serves 4

1 whole mullet, cleaned and scaled

salt and pepper

2 scallions, chopped

1 tsp grated fresh gingerroot

½ cup garlic wine vinegar

½ cup light soy sauce

3 tsp superfine sugar

dash of chili sauce

½ cup fish stock

1 green bell pepper, thinly sliced

1 large tomato, skinned, seeded and cut
  into thin strips

sliced tomato, to garnish

1 Rinse the fish inside and out and pat dry with paper towels.

2 Make 3 diagonal slits in the flesh on each side of the fish. Season with salt and pepper inside and out.

3 Place the fish on a heatproof plate and scatter the scallions and gingerroot over the top. Cover and steam for 10 minutes, or until the fish is cooked well through.

4

variation

Use fillets of fish for this recipe if preferred, and reduce the cooking time to 5-7 minutes.

cook's tip

Make sure that you cook the sauce for long enough so that it reduces and thickens slightly. It should not be too runny.

fusilli & smoked haddock with egg sauce

This quick, easy, and inexpensive dish would be ideal for a mid-week family supper.

1

Serves 4

2 tbsp butter, plus extra for oiling

1 lb smoked haddock fillets, cut into 4 slices

2¼ cups milk

¼ cup all-purpose flour

salt and pepper

pinch of freshly grated nutmeg

3 tbsp heavy cream

1 tbsp chopped fresh parsley

2 eggs, hard cooked and mashed to a pulp

4 cups dried fusilli

1 tbsp lemon juice

boiled new potatoes and beet

1 Thoroughly oil a Dutch oven with butter. Put the haddock in the Dutch oven and pour over the milk. Bake in a preheated oven at 400°F for about 15 minutes. Carefully pour the cooking liquid into a pitcher without breaking up the fish.

2 Melt the butter in a pan and stir in the flour. Whisk in the reserved cooking liquid. Season to taste with salt, pepper, and nutmeg. Stir in the cream, parsley, and mashed egg and cook, stirring constantly, for 2 minutes.

3 Meanwhile, bring a large pan of lightly salted water to the boil. Add the fusilli and lemon juice and cook until tender, but still firm to the bite.

4 Drain the pasta and spoon or tip it over the fish. Top with the sauce and return the Dutch oven to the oven for 10 minutes.

5 Serve with boiled new potatoes and beet.

variation

You can use any type of dried pasta for this casserole. Try penne, conchiglie, or rigatoni.

tuna steaks with fragrant spices & lime

Fresh tuna steaks are very meaty—they have a firm texture, yet the flesh is succulent. This recipe would be an impressive addition to a grill.

Serves 4

4 tuna steaks, 6 oz each

½ tsp finely grated lime peel

1 garlic clove, finely chopped

2 tsp olive oil

1 tsp ground cumin

1 tsp ground coriander

pepper

1 tbsp lime juice

2 tbsp chopped fresh cilantro

avocado relish (see Cook's Tip, below) and
    lime wedges, to serve

1

2

3

1 Trim the skin from the tuna steaks, rinse, and pat dry on absorbent paper towels.

2 In a small bowl, mix together the lime peel, garlic, olive oil, cumin, coriander, and pepper to make a paste.

3 Spread the paste thinly on both sides of the tuna. Heat a non-stick, ridged skillet until hot and press the tuna steaks into the pan to seal them. Lower the heat and cook for 5 minutes. Turn the fish over and cook for a further 4–5 minutes until the fish is cooked through. Drain on absorbent paper towels and transfer to a serving plate.

4 Sprinkle the lime juice and cilantro over the fish. Serve with freshly made avocado relish and lime wedges.

cook's tip

For low-fat avocado relish to serve with tuna, peel and remove the stone from one small ripe avocado. Toss in 1 tbsp lime juice. Mix in 1 tbsp freshly chopped cilantro and 1 small finely chopped red onion. Stir in some chopped fresh mango or a chopped medium tomato and season well.

spaghetti al tonno

The classic Italian combination of pasta and tuna is enhanced in this recipe with a delicious parsley sauce.

2

Serves 4

7 oz can tuna, drained

2 oz can anchovies, drained

1⅛ cups olive oil

1 cup roughly chopped flat leaf parsley

⅔ cup unsweetened yogurt

salt and pepper

1 lb dried spaghetti

2 tbsp butter

black olives, to garnish

crusty bread, to serve

4

1 Remove any bones from the tuna. Put the tuna into a food processor or blender, together with the anchovies, 1 cup of the olive oil, and the flat leaf parsley. Process until the sauce is smooth.

2 Spoon the unsweetened yogurt into the food processor or blender and process again for a few seconds to blend thoroughly. Season to taste with salt and pepper.

3 Bring a large pan of lightly salted water to the boil. Add the spaghetti and the remaining olive oil and cook until tender, but still firm to the bite.

4

4 Drain the spaghetti, return to the pan, and place over a medium heat. Add the butter and toss well to coat. Spoon in the sauce and quickly toss into the spaghetti, using 2 forks.

5 Remove the pan from the heat and divide the spaghetti between 4 warm individual serving plates. Garnish with the olives and serve immediately with warm, crusty bread.

genoese seafood risotto

The Genoese risotto is cooked in a different way from any of the other risottos. First, you cook the rice, then you prepare a sauce, then you mix the two together. The results are just as delicious though!

1

3

5

Serves 4

5 cups hot fish or chicken stock

12 oz risotto rice, washed

3 tbsp butter

2 garlic cloves, finely chopped

9 oz mixed seafood, preferably raw,
    such as shrimp, squid, mussels,
    and clams

2 tbsp chopped oregano, plus extra
    for garnishing

1¾ oz pecorino or Parmesan cheese, grated

1 In a large pan, bring the stock to the boil. Add the rice and cook for about 12 minutes, stirring, until the rice is tender or according to the instructions on the packet. Drain thoroughly, reserving any excess liquid.

2 Heat the butter in a large skillet and add the garlic, stirring.

3 Add the raw mixed seafood to the skillet and cook for 5 minutes. If the seafood is already cooked, cook for 2–3 minutes.

4 Stir the oregano into the seafood mixture in the skillet.

5 Add the cooked rice to the pan and cook for 2–3 minutes, stirring, or until hot. Add the reserved stock if the mixture gets too sticky.

6 Add the pecorino or Parmesan cheese and mix well.

7 Transfer the risotto to warm serving dishes, garnish with oregano and serve immediately.

cook's tip

The Genoese are excellent cooks, and they make particularly delicious fish dishes flavored with the local olive oil.

stir-fried gingered angler fish

This dish is a real treat and is perfect for special occasions. Angler fish has a tender flavor which is ideal with asparagus, chile, and ginger.

1

Serves 4

1 lb angler fish

1 tbsp freshly grated gingerroot

2 tbsp sweet chili sauce

1 tbsp corn oil

1 cup fine asparagus

3 scallions, sliced

1 tsp sesame oil

1 Using a sharp knife, slice the angler fish into thin flat rounds.

2 Mix the gingerroot with the chili sauce in a small bowl.

3 Brush the gingerroot and chili sauce mixture over the angler fish pieces.

4 Heat the corn oil in a large preheated wok.

5 Add the angler fish, asparagus, and scallions to the wok and stir-fry for about 5 minutes.

6 Remove the wok from the heat, drizzle the sesame oil over the stir-fry, and toss well to combine.

7 Transfer to warm serving plates and serve immediately.

3

5

variation

Angler fish is quite expensive, but it is well worth using it as it has a wonderful flavor and texture. At a push you could use cubes of chunky cod fillet instead.

cook's tip

Some recipes specify to grate gingerroot before it is cooked with other ingredients. To do this, just peel the flesh and rub it at a 45° angle up and down on the fine section of a metal grater, or use a special wooden or ceramic gingerroot grater.

trout with pineapple

Pineapple is widely used in Chinese cooking. The tartness of fresh pineapple complements fish particularly well.

Serves 4

4 trout fillets, skinned

2 tbsp vegetable oil

2 garlic cloves, cut into slivers

4 slices fresh pineapple, peeled and diced

1 celery stalk, sliced

1 tbsp light soy sauce

¼ cup fresh or unsweetened
   pineapple juice

⅔ cup fish stock

1 tsp cornstarch

2 tsp water

shredded celery leaves and fresh red chile
   strips, to garnish

1 Cut the trout fillets into strips. Heat 1 tablespoon of the vegetable oil in a preheated wok until almost smoking. Reduce the heat slightly, add the fish, and sauté for 2 minutes. Remove from the wok and set aside.

2 Add the remaining oil to the wok, reduce the heat, and add the garlic, pineapple, and celery. Stir-fry for 1–2 minutes.

3 Add the soy sauce, pineapple juice, and fish stock to the wok. Bring to the boil and cook, stirring, for 2–3 minutes, or until the sauce has reduced.

4 Blend the cornstarch with the water to form a paste and stir it into the wok. Bring the sauce to the boil and cook, stirring constantly, until the sauce thickens and clears.

5 Return the fish to the wok, and cook, stirring gently, until heated through. Transfer to a warmed serving dish and serve, garnished with shredded celery leaves and red chile strips.

cook's tip

Use canned pineapple instead of fresh pineapple if you wish, choosing slices in unsweetened, natural juice in preference to a syrup.

1

2

3

sea bass & macaroni with olive sauce

A favorite fish for chefs, the delicious sea bass is now becoming increasingly common in general and fish stores for family meals.

1

2

Serves 4

2 tbsp butter

4 shallots, finely chopped

2 tbsp capers

1½ cups pitted green olives, chopped

4 tbsp balsamic vinegar

1¼ cups fish stock

1¼ cups heavy cream

salt and pepper

juice of 1 lemon

1 lb dried macaroni

1 tbsp olive oil

8 x 4 oz sea bass medallions

lemon slices, shredded leek, and shredded
    carrot to garnish

1 To make the sauce, melt the butter in a skillet. Add the shallots and cook over a low heat for 4 minutes. Add the capers and olives and cook for a further 3 minutes.

2 Stir in the balsamic vinegar and fish stock, bring to the boil and reduce by half. Add the cream, stirring, and reduce again by half. Season to taste with salt and pepper and stir in the lemon juice. Remove the pan from the heat, set aside and keep warm.

3 Bring a large pan of lightly salted water to the boil. Add the pasta and olive oil and cook for about 12 minutes, until tender but still firm to the bite.

4 Meanwhile, lightly broil the sea bass medallions for 3–4 minutes on each side, until cooked through but still moist and delicate.

5 Drain the pasta and transfer to large individual serving dishes. Top the pasta with the fish medallions and pour the olive sauce over. Garnish with lemon slices, shredded leek, and shredded carrot and serve immediately.

2

The ideal ending to a meal is fresh fruit, topped with low-fat yogurt or fromage blanc. Fruit contains no fat and is sweet enough to need no extra sugar, but it is a valuable source of vitamins and fiber - ideal in every way for anyone who cares about their own and their family's health. There are, however, dozens of other ways in which fruit can be used as the basis for desserts and bakes, and thanks to modern transportation systems the range of unusual and exotic fruits available seems to expand every week. Experiment with some of these unfamiliar fruits in delicious warm desserts, sophisticated mousses and fools, and satisfying cakes, and use old favorites in enticing new ways.

deserts

sticky sesame bananas

These tasty morsels are a real treat. Pieces of banana are dipped in caramel and then sprinkled with a few sesame seeds.

Serves 4

4 ripe medium bananas

3 tbsp lemon juice

4 oz superfine sugar

4 tbsp cold water

2 tbsp sesame seeds

⅓ cup low-fat unsweetened yogurt

1 tbsp confectioners' sugar

1 tsp vanilla extract

shredded lemon and lime rind, to decorate

1

1 Peel the bananas and cut into 2 inch pieces. Place the banana pieces in a bowl, spoon over the lemon juice, and stir well to coat – this will help prevent the bananas from discoloring.

2 Place the sugar and water in a small pan and heat gently, stirring, until the sugar dissolves. Bring to the boil and cook for 5–6 minutes until the mixture turns golden-brown.

3 Meanwhile, drain the bananas and blot with absorbent paper towels to dry. Line a cookie sheet with baking parchment and arrange the bananas, well spaced out, on top.

3

4

4 When the caramel is ready, drizzle it over the bananas, working quickly because the caramel sets almost instantly. Sprinkle over the sesame seeds and leave to cool for 10 minutes.

5 Meanwhile, mix the unsweetened yogurt with the confectioners' sugar and vanilla extract.

6 Peel the bananas away from the paper and arrange on serving plates. Serve the yogurt as a dip, decorated with the shredded lemon and lime peel.

cook's tip

For best results, use a knife or a potato peeler to peel away thin strips of peel from the fruit, taking care not to include any bitter pith. Blanch the shreds in boiling water for 1 minute, then refresh in cold water.

pan-cooked apples in red wine

This simple combination of apples and raspberries cooked in red wine is a colorful and tempting dessert.

Serves 4

4 dessert apples

2 tbsp lemon juice

1½ oz low-fat spread

2 oz light muscovado sugar

1 small orange

1 cinnamon stick, broken

¼ cup red wine

8 oz raspberries, hulled and thawed if frozen

sprigs of fresh mint, to decorate

variation

Experiment with other soft fruit, such as blackberries or redcurrants. You may need to add more sugar if you use currants as they are not as sweet as raspberries.

1

5

1 Peel and core the apples, then cut them into thick wedges. Place the apples in a bowl and toss in the lemon juice to prevent the fruit from discoloring.

2 In a skillet, gently melt the low-fat spread over a low heat, add the sugar, and stir to form a paste.

3 Stir the apple wedges into the pan and cook, stirring, for 2 minutes until well coated in the sugar paste.

4

4 Using a vegetable peeler, pare off a few strips of orange peel. Add the orange peel to the pan along with the cinnamon pieces. Extract the juice from the orange and pour into the pan with the red wine. Bring to the boil, then simmer for 10 minutes, stirring.

5 Add the raspberries to the pan and cook for 5 minutes until the apples are tender.

6 Discard the orange peel and cinnamon pieces. Transfer the apple and raspberry mixture to a serving plate together with the wine sauce. Decorate with a sprig of fresh mint and serve hot.

grilled fruit platter with lime "butter"

This delicious variation of a hot fruit salad includes wedges of tropical fruits, dusted with dark brown, treacly sugar, and a pinch of spice before broiling.

Serves 4

1 baby pineapple

1 ripe papaya

1 ripe mango

2 kiwi fruit

4 finger bananas

4 tbsp dark rum

1 tsp ground allspice

2 tbsp lime juice

4 tbsp dark muscovado sugar

LIME "BUTTER"

2 oz low-fat spread

½ tsp finely grated lime peel

1 tbsp confectioners' sugar

variation

Serve with a light sauce of 1¼ cups tropical fruit juice thickened with 2 tsp arrowroot.

1

3

5

1 Quarter the pineapple, trimming away most of the leaves, and place in a shallow dish. Peel the papaya, cut it in half, and scoop out the seeds. Cut the flesh into thick wedges and place in the same dish as the pineapple.

2 Peel the mango, cut either side of the smooth, central flat stone, and remove the stone. Slice the flesh into thick wedges. Peel the kiwi fruit and cut in half. Peel the bananas. Add all of these fruits to the dish.

3 Sprinkle over the rum, allspice and lime juice, cover, and leave at room temperature for 30 minutes, turning occasionally, to allow the flavors to develop.

4 Meanwhile, make the butter. Place the low-fat spread in a small bowl and beat in the lime peel and sugar until well mixed. Leave to chill until required.

5 Preheat the broiler to hot. Drain the fruit, reserving the juices, and arrange in the broiler pan. Sprinkle with the sugar and broil for 3–4 minutes until hot, bubbling, and beginning to char.

6 Transfer the fruit to a serving plate and spoon over the juices. Serve with the lime butter.

toffee fruit kabobs

Serve these fruit kabobs with a sticky toffee sauce. They are perfect for fall celebrations such as Hallowe'en.

1

Serves 4

2 dessert apples, cored and cut into
    wedges

2 firm pears, cored and cut into wedges

juice of ½ lemon

1 oz light muscovado sugar

¼ tsp ground allspice

1 oz unsalted butter, melted

SAUCE

4½ oz butter

3½ oz light muscovado sugar

6 tbsp heavy cream

1 Toss the apple and pears in the lemon juice to prevent any discoloration.

2 Mix the sugar and allspice together and sprinkle over the fruit.

3 Thread the fruit pieces on to skewers.

4 To make the toffee sauce, place the butter and sugar in a pan and heat, stirring gently, until the butter has melted and the sugar has dissolved.

5 Add the cream to the pan and bring to the boil. Boil for 1–2 minutes, then set aside to cool slightly.

6 Meanwhile, place the fruit kabobs over hot coals and grill for about 5 minutes, turning and basting frequently with the melted butter, until the fruit is just tender.

7 Transfer the fruit kabobs to warm serving plates and serve with the slightly cooled toffee sauce.

variation

Sprinkle the fruit kabobs with
chopped walnuts or pecan nuts
before serving, if you wish.

2

5

rich chocolate loaf

Although quite rich, this chocolate loaf is very simple to make and can be served as a tea-time treat as well as for dessert.

Makes 16 slices

2¼ oz almonds

5½ oz semisweet chocolate

6 tbsp butter, unsalted

7¼ oz tin sweetened condensed milk

2 tsp cinnamon

2¼ oz amaretti cookies, broken

1¼ oz dried no-need-to-soak apricots,
   roughly chopped

cook's tip

To melt chocolate, first break it into manageable pieces. The smaller the pieces, the quicker it will melt.

1

2

3

cook's tip

When baking or cooking with fat, butter has the finest flavor. If possible, it is best to use unsalted butter as an ingredient in puddings and desserts, unless stated otherwise in the recipe.

1 Line a 1½ lb loaf pan with a sheet of kitchen foil.

2 Using a sharp knife, roughly chop the almonds.

3 Place the chocolate, butter, milk, and cinnamon in a heavy-based pan. Heat gently over a low heat for 3–4 minutes, stirring with a wooden spoon, until the chocolate has melted. Beat the mixture well.

4 Stir the almonds, cookies, and apricots into the chocolate mixture in the pan, stirring with a wooden spoon, until well mixed.

5 Pour the mixture into the prepared pan and leave to chill in the refrigerator for about 1 hour or until set.

6 Cut the rich chocolate loaf into slices to serve.

red fruits with foaming sauce

A colorful combination of soft fruits, served with a frothy marshmallow sauce, is an ideal dessert when summer fruits are in season.

1

2

3

Serves 4

8 oz redcurrants, washed and trimmed, thawed if frozen

8 oz cranberries

3 oz light muscovado sugar

¾ cup unsweetened apple juice

1 cinnamon stick, broken

10½ oz small strawberries, washed, hulled and halved

SAUCE

8 oz raspberries, thawed if frozen

2 tbsp fruit cordial

3½ oz marshmallows

1 Place the redcurrants, cranberries, and sugar in a pan. Pour in the apple juice and add the cinnamon stick. Bring the mixture to the boil and simmer gently for 10 minutes until the fruit has just softened.

2 Stir the strawberries into the cranberry and sugar mixture and mix well. Transfer the mixture to a bowl, cover, and leave to chill in the refrigerator for about 1 hour. Remove and discard the cinnamon stick.

3 Just before serving, make the sauce. Place the raspberries and fruit cordial in a small pan, bring to a boil, and simmer for 2–3 minutes until the fruit is just beginning to soften. Stir the marshmallows into the raspberry mixture and heat through, stirring, until the marshmallows begin to melt.

4 Transfer the fruit salad to serving bowls. Spoon over the raspberry and marshmallow sauce and serve.

variation

This sauce is delicious poured over low-fat ice cream. For an extra-colorful sauce, replace the raspberries with an assortment of summer berries.

peaches in white wine

A very simple but incredibly pleasing dessert, which is especially good for a dinner party on a hot summer day.

1

Serves 4

4 large ripe peaches

2 tbsp confectioners' sugar, sifted

pared peel and juice of 1 orange

¾ cup medium or sweet white wine, chilled

1 Using a sharp knife, halve the peaches, remove the stones, and discard them. Peel the peaches if you prefer. Slice the peaches into thin wedges.

2 Place the peach wedges in a glass serving bowl and sprinkle the sugar over.

1

3 Using a sharp knife, pare the peel from the orange. Cut the orange peel into matchsticks, place them in a bowl of cold water and set aside.

4 Squeeze the juice from the orange and pour over the peaches together with the wine.

5 Leave the peaches to marinate and chill in the refrigerator for at least 1 hour.

6 Remove the orange peel from the cold water and pat dry with paper towels.

7 Garnish the peaches with the strips of orange peel and serve immediately.

cook's tip

There is absolutely no need to use expensive wine in this recipe, so it can be quite economical to make.

cook's tip

The best way to pare the peel thinly from citrus fruits is to use a potato peeler.

3

baked bananas

The orange-flavored cream can be prepared in advance but do not make up the banana packets until just before you need to grill them—they take only a few momentsto get ready.

Serves 4

4 bananas

2 passion fruit

4 tbsp orange juice

4 tbsp orange-flavored liqueur

⅔ cup heavy cream

3 tbsp confectioners' sugar

2 tbsp orange-flavored liqueur

1 Peel the bananas and place each one on to a sheet of kitchen foil.

2 Cut the passion fruit in half and squeeze the juice of each half over each banana. Spoon over the orange juice and liqueur.

3 Fold the kitchen foil over the top of the bananas to enclose the bananas completely.

4 Grill the bananas over hot coals for about 10 minutes or until the bananas are just tender.

5 To make the orange-flavored cream, pour the heavy cream into a mixing bowl and sprinkle over the confectioners' sugar. Whisk the mixture until it is standing in soft peaks. Carefully fold in the orange-flavored liqueur and leave to chill in the refrigerator until required.

6 Transfer the foil parcels to warm, individual serving plates. Open out the foil packets at the table and then serve with the orange-flavored cream.

variation

Leave the bananas in their skins for a really quick dessert. Split the banana skins and pop in 1-2 cubes of chocolate. Wrap the bananas in kitchen foil and grill for 10 minutes, or until the chocolate just melts.

baked pears with cinnamon & brown sugar

This simple recipe is deliciously warming. Serve hot with low-fat custard, or allow to cool and serve chilled with fromage blanc or yogurt.

Serves 4

4 ripe pears

2 tbsp lemon juice

4 tbsp light muscovado sugar

1 tsp ground cinnamon

2 oz low-fat spread

low-fat custard, to serve

lemon peel, finely grated, to decorate

1

2

3

1 Preheat the oven to 400°F. Core and peel the pears, then slice them in half lengthwise and brush all over with the lemon juice to prevent the pears from discoloring. Place the pears, cored side down, in a small non-stick roasting pan.

2 Place the sugar, cinnamon, and low-fat spread in a small pan and heat gently, stirring, until the sugar has melted. Keep the heat low to stop too much water evaporating from the low-fat spread as it gets hot. Spoon the mixture over the pears.

3 Bake for 20–25 minutes or until the pears are tender and golden, occasionally spooning the sugar mixture over the fruit during the cooking time.

4 To serve, heat the custard until it is very hot and spoon over the bases of 4 warm dessert plates. Arrange 2 pear halves on each plate. Decorate with grated lemon peel and serve.

variation

This recipe also works well if you use cooking apples. For alternative flavors, replace the cinnamon with ground ginger and serve the pears sprinkled with chopped stem ginger in syrup. Alternatively, use ground allspice and spoon over some warmed dark rum to serve.

brown sugar pavlovas

This simple combination of fudge meringue topped with yogurt and raspberries is the perfect finale to any meal.

Serves 4

2 large egg whites

1 tsp cornstarch

1 tsp raspberry vinegar

3½ oz light muscovado sugar, crushed free
  of lumps

2 tbsp redcurrant jelly

2 tbsp unsweetened orange juice

¾ cup low-fat unsweetened yogurt

6 oz raspberries, thawed if frozen

rose-scented geranium leaves, to decorate

1

1 Preheat the oven to 300°F. Line
  a large cookie sheet with baking
parchment. In a large, grease-free bowl,
whisk the egg whites until very stiff and
dry. Fold in the cornstarch and vinegar.

2 Gradually whisk in the sugar, a
  spoonful at a time, until the mixture
is thick and glossy.

3 Divide the mixture into 4 and spoon
  on to the cookie sheet, spaced well
apart. Smooth each into a round, about
4 inch across, and bake in the oven for
40–45 minutes until browned and crisp.
Leave to cool on the baking tray.

2

3

4 Place the redcurrant jelly and
  orange juice in a small pan and
heat, stirring, until melted. Leave to cool
for 10 minutes.

5 Meanwhile, using a palette knife,
  carefully remove each pavlova from
the baking parchment and transfer to a
serving plate. Top with unsweetened
yogurt and raspberries.

6 Spoon over the redcurrant jelly
  mixture to glaze. Decorate and serve.

variation

Make a large pavlova by
forming the meringue into
a circle, measuring 7 inches
across, on a lined baking
sheet and bake for 1 hour.

baked apples with blackberries

This winter dessert is a classic dish. Large, fluffy apples are hollowed out and filled with spices, almonds, and blackberries. Serve hot with low-fat custard.

1

Serves 4

4 medium-sized cooking apples

1 tbsp lemon juice

3½ oz prepared blackberries, thawed
    if frozen

½ oz slivered almonds

½ tsp ground allspice

½ tsp finely grated lemon peel

2 tbsp brown crystal sugar

1¼ cups ruby port

1 cinnamon stick, broken

2 tsp cornstarch blended with 2 tbsp
    cold water

low-fat custard, to serve

2

3

1 Preheat the oven to 400°F. Wash and dry the apples. Using a small sharp knife, make a shallow cut through the skin around the middle of each apple —this will help the apples to cook through.

2 Core the apples, brush the centers with the lemon juice to prevent browning, and stand in a shallow ovenproof dish.

3 In a bowl, mix together the blackberries, almonds, allspice, lemon peel, and sugar. Using a teaspoon, spoon the mixture into the center of each apple.

4 Pour the port into the dish, add the cinnamon stick, and bake the apples in the oven for 35–40 minutes or until tender and soft. Drain the cooking juices into a pan and keep the apples warm.

5 Discard the cinnamon and add the cornstarch mixture to the cooking juices. Heat, stirring, until thickened.

6 Heat the custard until very hot. Pour the sauce over the apples and serve with the custard.

variation

Use raspberries instead of blackberries and, if you prefer, replace the port with unsweetened orange juice.

almond trifles

Amaretti cookies made with ground almonds have a high fat content. This recipe uses cookies made from apricot kernels, which have a lower fat content.

1

3

variation

Try this trifle with assorted summer fruits. If they are a frozen mix, use them frozen and allow them to thaw so that the juices soak into the cookie base — it will taste delicious.

Serves 4

8 Amaretti di Saronno cookies

4 tbsp brandy or Amaretti liqueur

8 oz raspberries, thawed if frozen

1¼ cups low-fat custard

1¼ cups low-fat unsweetened yogurt

1 tsp almond extract

½ oz toasted almonds, slivered

1 tsp cocoa powder

1 Place the cookies in a mixing bowl and using a rolling pin, carefully crush the cookies into small pieces.

2 Divide the crushed cookies among 4 serving glasses. Sprinkle over the brandy or liqueur and leave to stand for about 30 minutes to allow the cookies to soften.

3 Top the layer of cookies with a layer of raspberries, reserving a few raspberries for decoration, and spoon over enough custard to just cover.

4 Mix the unsweetened yogurt with the almond extract and spoon over the custard. Leave to chill in the refrigerator for about 30 minutes.

4

5 Just before serving, sprinkle over the toasted almonds and dust with cocoa powder. Decorate with the reserved raspberries and serve at once.

fruit & fiber layers

A good, hearty dessert, guaranteed to fill you up. Use your own favorite dried fruits in the compote, and eat it with a clear conscience!

1

Serves 4

4 oz no-need-to-soak dried apricots

4 oz no-need-to-soak dried prunes

4 oz no-need-to-soak dried peaches

2 oz dried apple

1 oz dried cherries

2 cups unsweetened apple juice

6 cardamom pods

6 cloves

1 cinnamon stick, broken

1¼ cups low-fat natural yogurt

4 oz crunchy oat cereal

apricot slices, to decorate

3

4

1 To make the fruit compote, place the dried apricots, prunes, peaches, apples, and cherries in a pan and pour in the apple juice.

2 Add the cardamom pods, cloves, and cinnamon stick to the pan, bring to the boil and simmer for 10–15 minutes until the fruits are plump and tender.

3 Allow the mixture to cool completely in the pan, transfer the mixture to a bowl, and leave to chill in the refrigerator for 1 hour. Remove and discard the spices from the fruits.

4 Spoon the compote into 4 dessert glasses, layering it alternately with yogurt and oat cereal, finishing with the oat cereal on top.

5 Decorate each dessert with slices of apricot and serve at once.

cook's tip

There are many dried fruits available, including mangoes and pears, some of which need soaking, so read the instructions on the packet before use. Also, check the ingredients label, because several types of dried fruit have added sugar or are rolled in sugar, and this will affect the sweetness of the dish you use them in.

tropical fruit fool

Fruit fools are always popular, and this lightly tangy version will be no exception. Use your favorite fruits in this recipe if you prefer.

1

Serves 4

1 medium ripe mango

2 kiwi fruit

1 medium banana

2 tbsp lime juice

¼ tsp finely grated lime peel, plus extra
   to decorate

2 medium egg whites

15 oz can low-fat custard

¼ tsp vanilla extract

2 passion fruits

2

4

1 Peel the mango and slice either side of the smooth, flat central stone. Roughly chop the flesh and blend the fruit in a food processor or blender until smooth. Alternatively, mash with a fork.

2 Peel the kiwi fruit, chop the flesh into small pieces, and place in a bowl. Peel and chop the banana and add to the bowl. Toss all of the fruit in the lime juice and peel and mix well.

3 In a grease-free bowl, whisk the egg whites until stiff and then gently fold in the custard and vanilla extract until mixed.

4 In 4 tall glasses, alternately layer the chopped fruit, mango purée, and custard mixture, finishing with the custard on top. Leave to chill in the refrigerator for 20 minutes.

5 Halve the passion fruits, scoop out the seeds, and spoon the passion fruit over the fruit fools. Decorate each serving with the extra lime peel and serve.

orange & grapefruit salad

Sliced citrus fruits with a delicious almond and honey dressing make an unusual and refreshing dessert that will liven up the palate.

Serves 4

2 grapefruit, ruby or plain

4 oranges

pared peel and juice of 1 lime

4 tbsp clear honey

2 tbsp warm water

1 sprig of mint, roughly chopped

1¾ oz chopped walnuts

1 Using a sharp knife, slice the top and bottom from the grapefruits, then slice away the rest of the skin and pith.

2 Cut between each segment of the grapefruit to remove the fleshy part only.

3 Using a sharp knife, slice the top and bottom from the oranges, then slice away the rest of the skin and pith.

4 Cut between each segment of the oranges to remove the fleshy part. Add to the grapefruit.

5 Place the lime peel, 2 tablespoons of lime juice, the honey, and the warm water in a small bowl. Whisk with a fork to mix the dressing.

6 Pour the dressing over the segmented fruit, add the chopped mint, and mix well. Leave to chill in the refrigerator for 2 hours for the flavors to mingle.

7 Place the chopped walnuts on a cookie sheet. Lightly toast the walnuts under a preheated medium broiler for 2–3 minutes until browned.

8 Sprinkle the toasted walnuts over the fruit and serve.

1

2

5

variation

Instead of the walnuts, you could sprinkle toasted almonds, cashew nuts, hazelnuts, or pecans over the fruit, if you prefer.

citrus meringue crush

This is an excellent way to use up left-over meringue shells. It is very simple to prepare, yet tastes very luxurious. Serve with a spoonful of tangy fruit sauce.

Serves 4

8 ready-made meringue nests

1¼ cups low-fat unsweetened yogurt

½ tsp finely grated orange peel

½ tsp finely grated lemon peel

½ tsp finely grated lime peel

2 tbsp orange liqueur or unsweetened
 orange juice

sliced kumquat and grated lime peel,
 to decorate

SAUCE

2 oz kumquats

8 tbsp unsweetened orange juice

2 tbsp lemon juice

2 tbsp lime juice

2 tbsp water

2–3 tsp superfine sugar

1 tsp cornstarch mixed with 1 tbsp water

1

2

3

1 Place the meringues in a clean plastic bag, seal the bag, and using a rolling pin, crush the meringues into small pieces. Transfer the crushed meringues to a mixing bowl.

2 Stir the yogurt, grated citrus peels, and the liqueur or juice into the crushed meringue. Spoon the mixture into 4 mini-basins, smooth over the tops, and freeze for 1½–2 hours until firm.

3 Meanwhile, make the sauce. Thinly slice the kumquats and place them in a small pan with the fruit juices and water. Bring gently to the boil and then simmer over a low heat for 3–4 minutes until the kumquats have just softened.

4 Sweeten with sugar to taste, stir in the cornstarch mixture and cook, stirring, until thickened. Pour into a small bowl, cover the surface with a layer of plastic wrap and allow to cool – the film will help prevent a skin forming. Leave to chill until required.

5 To serve, dip the meringue basins in hot water for 5 seconds or until they loosen, and turn on to serving plates. Spoon over a little sauce, decorate with slices of kumquat and lime peel, and serve immediately.

vanilla ice cream

Italy is synonymous with ice cream. This home-made version of real vanilla ice cream is absolutely delicious and so easy to make.

Serves 4-6

2½ cups heavy cream

1 vanilla pod

pared peel of 1 lemon

4 eggs, beaten

2 egg, yolks

6 oz superfine sugar

cook's tip

To make tutti frutti ice cream, soak 3½ oz mixed dried fruit, such as sultanas, cherries, apricots, candied peel, and pineapple, in 2 tbsp of Marsala or sweet sherry for 20 minutes. Follow the method for vanilla ice cream, omitting the vanilla pod, and stir in the Marsala or sherry-soaked fruit in step 5, just before freezing.

1

3

5

1 Place the cream in a heavy-based pan and heat gently, whisking. Add the vanilla pod, lemon peel, eggs, and egg yolks and heat until the mixture reaches just below boiling point.

2 Reduce the heat and cook for 8–10 minutes, whisking the mixture continuously, until thickened.

3 Stir the sugar into the cream mixture, set aside, and leave to cool.

4 Strain the cream mixture through a strainer.

5 Slit open the vanilla pod, scoop out the tiny black seeds, and stir them into the cream.

6 Pour the mixture into a shallow freezing container with a lid and freeze overnight until set. Serve when required.

cook's tip

Ice cream is one of the traditional dishes of Italy. Everyone eats it and there are numerous gelato stalls selling a wide variety of flavors, usually in a cone. It is also serve in scoops and even sliced!

granita

A delightful end to a meal or a refreshing way to cleanse the palate between courses, granitas need to be served very quickly.

1

Serves 4

LEMON GRANITA

3 lemons

⅞ cup lemon juice

3½ oz superfine sugar

2¼ cups cold water

COFFEE GRANITA

2 tbsp instant coffee

2 tbsp sugar

2 tbsp hot water

2½ cups cold water

2 tbsp rum or brandy

1

2

cook's tip

If you would prefer a non-alcoholic version of the coffee granita, simply omit the rum or brandy and add extra instant coffee instead.

1 To make lemon granita, finely grate the lemon peel. Place the lemon peel, juice, and superfine sugar in a pan. Bring the mixture to the boil and leave to simmer for 5-6 minutes or until thick and syrupy. Leave to cool.

2 Once cooled, stir in the cold water and pour into a shallow freezer container with a lid. Freeze the granita for 4–5 hours, stirring occasionally to break up the ice. Serve as a palate cleanser between dinner courses.

3 To make coffee granita, place the coffee and sugar in a bowl and pour over the hot water, stirring until dissolved.

4 Stir in the cold water and rum or brandy.

5 Pour the mixture into a shallow freezer container with a lid. Freeze the granita for at least 6 hours, stirring every 1–2 hours in order to create a grainy texture. Serve with cream after dinner, if you wish.

index